Anyone wanting to understand the power of collective experience in constructing a better world will find this book invaluable. It vividly illustrates the transformative power of learning communities constructed by older black women, posing a much needed challenge both to conventional ideas of community organizing and to policy and research around communities and diversity. Etienne's writing is theoretically informed and grounded in powerful narratives, which present a complex weave of past and present aspirations, struggles and social responsibilities. It reveals how creative movements to pursue social change can be constructed differently through the solidarity of older black w⌐⌐⌐⌐'s shared experience.

Dr Linda Milbourne, Associate Fellow, University of Birn

GW00645302

This is no ordinary book on aging, migra
and empowering story of the wisdom oi a⌐⌐⌐ ⌐
lifelong struggle. Paying tribute to the African Caribbean women of her mother's generation, Etienne sensitively reveals the power of shared 'other ways of knowing' that lie at the heart of their 'matriarchal learning hubs'. Her careful crafting of their rhythmic voices into scenes in a play is a tribute to the black womanist philosophy she herself has been gifted by these women. Etienne puts Paulo Freire's *Pedagogy of the Oppressed* into action, showing us the transformative power of education if it is grounded in generosity, love and experience. A must read for educationalists and social scientists who want a better world.

Heidi Safia Mirza, Professor of Race, Faith and Culture, Goldsmiths College, University of London; Author of *Young, Female and Black* (Routledge); *Race, Gender and Educational Desire: How Black Women Succeed and Fail* (Routledge)

This book breaks new ground by making central the experiences of African Caribbean, older women – a group usually rendered silent in social theory and research. It foregrounds their voices and situates them as active, lifelong learners whose narratives illuminate their creativity in negotiating structural constraints and contributing to their communities. The word innovative is frequently overused, but this book forges new and engaging ways of bringing together the author's reflexivity and the drama of the women's everyday lives. It deserves to be widely read.

Ann Phoenix, Professor of Psychosocial Studies, UCL Institute of Education

This book is dedicated to my late mother, Veronica Neola Charlemagne Etienne, who instilled in me a determination to succeed.

It is also dedicated to Lloyd, for his tireless patience and staunch support throughout the writing of the book, and to Stuart for keeping me grounded.

Finally, this book is also for all those second- and third-generation African Caribbean sisters steeped in the ever present struggle to flourish in the academy.

Learning in Womanist Ways

To Agnes ready my
enjoy unwomanist ways
lots of love
Jan.
24/5/16

Learning in Womanist Ways

Narratives of first-generation African Caribbean women

Jan Etienne

is an imprint of

First published in 2016 by the UCL Institute of Education Press, University College London, 20 Bedford Way, London WC1H 0AL

www.ucl-ioe-press.com

British Library Cataloguing in Publication Data:
A catalogue record for this publication is available from the British Library

ISBNs
978-1-85856-778-5 (paperback)
978-1-85856-779-2 (PDF eBook)
978-1-85856-780-8 (ePub eBook)
978-1-85856-781-5 (Kindle eBook)

Every effort has been made to trace copyright holders and to obtain their permission for the use of copyright material. The publisher apologizes for any errors or omissions and would be grateful if notified of any corrections that should be incorporated in future reprints or editions of this book.

The opinions expressed in this publication are those of the author and do not necessarily reflect the views of the UCL Institute of Education, University College London.

Typeset by Quadrant Infotech (India) Pvt Ltd
Printed by CPI Group (UK) Ltd, Croydon, CR0 4YY

Contents

Acknowledgements

I thank all the many first-generation African Caribbean (West Indian) women who took part in my research study and who are represented in the various acts in this book. I particularly want to thank Tannis for her inspiration and Nicole for her hard work on the proofs. I owe a debt of gratitude to Dr Linda Milbourne and Professor John Annette for their dedication and guidance. And I thank Dr Gillian Klein at Trentham Books for her excellent support and commitment to my area of study.

About the author

Jan Etienne holds a PhD from the Department of Social Policy and Education at Birkbeck, University of London, and an MSc from the School for Policy Studies at the University of Bristol. She lectures in the School of Social Sciences, History and Philosophy at Birkbeck, University of London, on modules such as 'Social Justice and Public Policy', 'Approaches to Social Conflict' and 'Understanding the Social World'.

Jan's publications include: 'Lifelong learning in later years: Choices and constraints for older women' (2011) in Jackson et al. (eds) *Gendered Choices: Learning, work, identities in lifelong learning*; 'Beyond the home: Informal learning and community practice for older women' (2010) in Jackson, S. (ed.) *Innovations in Lifelong Learning: Critical perspectives on diversity, participation and vocational learning*; and 'Black managers in further education: Career hopes and hesitations' (2006) with Fiona Mackay, *Educational Management, Administration and Leadership*, 34 (1).

Prior to a career in teaching, Jan worked as a women's rights officer in the London Borough of Hackney, a race relations adviser in the London Borough of Haringey and as head of the Housing Equalities Unit in the London Borough of Hammersmith and Fulham. She is a former local elected member and chair of the Education Committee in the London Borough of Brent and an Executive Governor of Ruskin College, Oxford.

Foreword

John Field

Jan Etienne's study of older African Caribbean women learners comes as a refreshing counter-blast to the usual fare. It isn't just that this group is rarely addressed by education researchers, even those few who go beyond the limited worlds of school and university; she also brings a fresh analytical approach to her subject. Drawing on the narratives of over 100 learners, all first-generation migrants to Britain, she examines the ways in which learning interacts with and is embedded in other dimensions of everyday life, from friendship and family networks through to their wider communities, physical and imagined, and she asks how the benefits of their learning then feed back into their own lives and those of their communities.

Narrative research imposes a heavy burden on the researcher. Interviewing 100 women across 11 UK cities, Etienne has accumulated a body of evidence containing rich variety and multiple perspectives, which reveals the vast complexity of the participants' worlds. She invites us to understand her evidence as revealing the 'womanist ways' in which these older black women pass on their knowledge, share ways of learning and provoke one another to explore new ideas and information. That is to say, she draws on feminist epistemologies that are informed by an Africanist recognition of multiple, polyrhythmic realities, as well as an awareness of what we might call the 'mundane sociologies' of everyday lives.

To take us into their world, Etienne employs dramatic devices that position us and her in relation to the actors as they tell their stories, and she illuminates some key points with verse. The upshot is a major contribution to educational research and to our understanding of migrant experiences; it is also a terrific read. Etienne reports on the ways in which the women – women of her mother's generation – addressed her, reprimanded her, corrected her and teased her, often in a language that certainly I cannot easily understand, and that perhaps they expected the researcher to find puzzling. Yet as she shows, each of these exercises in 'sisterly sparring', apparently designed to put the researcher (highly-educated, second generation, a university academic) in her place, also reveals much about their sense of who they are, as individual women and as members of multiple communities.

The core of the book, though, lies in its examination of everyday learning across different areas of the women's lives, and its interplay with their varying and sometimes overlapping forms of civic and community engagement. Some key messages for policy emerge along with the rich research data. For example, Etienne follows the ways in which several of her participants contribute with growing confidence and knowledge to public-sector-led regeneration initiatives, challenging attempts to render them invisible, and exercising real – if still constrained – influence. She also considers the role of learning in relation to health, a key issue for a group of people who by virtue of age and condition are typically at risk from certain illnesses.

Etienne's conclusions reach far beyond the limits of older African Caribbean women, though she certainly justifies her decision to focus on this group. She reminds us of the importance of generation: her participants were schooled within a rigid colonial framework of didactic instruction, encountering adult learning as a kind of liberation in which they acted not as passive receptacles but as creative agents for change. In a pattern that will be familiar to many who have worked with older adults, she tells us that this group of older women resist the new labels that others – including Jan Etienne when introducing her research topic to them – believed suitable (they particularly resent being called 'African', as in 'African Caribbean', for example). She shows, and explores, the dense web of personal relationships and ties that both support and shape that learning, and in turn are re-shaped by it. She shows the importance of respect and recognition in motivating the women to learn, and to share their experiences of learning. Her 'womanist' approach helps her identify what she calls 'black matriarchal learning hubs', a concept that I hope she – and others – will continue to examine in the future. She poses important questions about the concept of 'inclusion', relating it to issues of power and control, and we can link this in turn with her remarks about the double-edged nature of social capital.

Learning in Womanist Ways makes an important new contribution to educational research. It particularly extends our understanding of learning in later life, and it shows us something of what happens when migrants cease to be migrants and start to 'age in place' (somehow I suspect the women would hate that term as well). It emphatically demonstrates that 'aging in place' is an active process in which people re-make their own communities and help to shape the wider world around them. It explores in detail the role of learning in that active process of re-making identities and shaping institutions, as well as presenting us with the consequences of existing structures and inherited identities for learning. And it is a sheer joy to read. What more could you ask for?

John Field, University of Stirling

Chapter 1

Introduction

How does it feel to be older, black and female and have the desire for purposeful learning? This book engages with the narratives of black women over the age of 50 who are prioritizing learning for a purpose. In dramatized acts, presented in vivid Caribbean theatrical manner, first-generation African Caribbean women describe their learning motivations and argue, often ruthlessly, on the way forward for the younger generation. While reflecting on their education, the women provide revealing insights into their learning lives – lives filled with experiences of injustice, private shame and humiliation, as they look forward to a brighter, more qualified, purposeful future.

The book captures the nature of Caribbean womanist learning, a black feminist perspective where women provoke, coerce and challenge each other, often in whimsical ways, and where formidable attitudes and the originality of West Indian colloquialisms generate confidences and inspire others. In theatrical representations, the book explores the benefits of learning for a group of women who are living at a time when being black, female and older is often associated with deteriorating health, poverty and isolation (Smith *et al.*, 2000; Platt, 2007; Afshar *et al.*, 2002b). The book is about lifelong learning and active citizenship and is based on my PhD thesis, a contemporary narrative study (Chase, 2008; Clandinin, 2006) conducted across 11 UK cities and involving over 100 women learners.

The work reveals the social and cultural identities brought to lifelong learning, illustrating solidarity in Caribbean sisterhood as black women find ways to rise above the challenges presented by learning in a climate of uncertainty in which cuts to public services impact on their daily lives. It illustrates how learning in later years can transform traditional community spaces into thriving learning hubs in an attempt to increase social capital, defined by Field and Spence as 'the existence of networks, norms and levels of trust that promote collective action between members of a given social grouping' (2000: 32). Social capital concerns the value and importance placed on social networks and the resources derived from such networks for the collective benefit of the wider community. With regard to the women in this study, their relationships with others (that I refer to as 'bridging' social capital) and their creativity (as they engage with outsiders to pursue their various project activities) provide a rich source of social capital (Alfred, 2009) that impacts on the wider community.

According to Putnam (2000), social capital is built particularly effectively through civic engagement. As active citizens (Crick, 2000a) the women work alongside others (trainers, local councillors, regeneration board members and others) and experience mutual support while they pursue their objectives. Such interaction and participation in the various local initiatives described in this book have the potential to increase local contacts, creating social networks that are underpinned by shared values. Social networks of this kind can produce high levels of social trust, which in turn fosters cooperation between the women and with those whom they acknowledge as influential in promoting their aims. In the lives of the women in this study, social capital can develop transformative power (Kilpatrick *et al.*, 2003) with which, together, they are able to develop a form of 'bonding' social capital that reinforces solidarity and sisterhood and helps them challenge the status quo. Social capital can therefore bring a new lease of life to older black women, for whom formal education was a luxury to which they had limited access when they were younger.

And while the book concerns older black women learners it speaks to all adult learners who are seeking to reclaim their education and make up for lost time. It is written for those who faced barriers to their education but now feel motivated to study in an effort to add new meaningful dimensions to their lives. The book is written also for practitioners and policymakers committed to removing obstacles to learning in later life and for all those who see education as a basic human right and as a way of promoting freedom and justice in this unequal world.

Lifelong learning has been described as a continuum of the learning process that takes place at all levels – formal, non-formal and informal. It is a broad and ambiguous concept embracing education that is flexible, diverse and available at different times and places and pursued throughout life (Field, 2006a). It has been explored in many different ways and by many different commentators (Coffield, 1997; Soulsby, 2000; McGivney, 1999; Griffin, 2000) and it offers potential second and third chances to generations of learners who, for one reason or another, missed out on what they consider to be appropriate formal education. A great deal is known about the benefits of lifelong learning (Mayo, 2000; Aldridge and Tuckett, 2002; Schuller *et al.*, 2004; Withnall, 2002; Jackson, 2007; McNair, 2009), but not much is known about the benefits of lifelong learning for older black women.

In parallel with other older learners, a focus on economic purposes can be misplaced as older black women's learning aims are not necessarily about entering the job market or improving their employment prospects but rather about participating in learning opportunities as a way of improving the quality of their lives.

In the UK, lifelong learning is typically understood as including community learning (adult learning and community classes); further education; higher education; the use of libraries, archives and information services; and work-based learning. However, this understanding would limit its meaning only to these potentially concrete settings. There are boundaries and overlaps between: a) formal/non-formal/informal learning; b) Freire's differentiation (1970, 1972) of democratizing learning; c) using lifelong learning contexts to fulfil formal citizenship duties or work-related skills; and d) participation in social networks.

The type of lifelong learning I explored in my research is primarily located within social networks, where learners are interacting with others within voluntary and community organizations (Adelson, 2000) and through membership of faith and social groups. In more recent terminology, it may, therefore, be construed as informal learning. Often those participating in informal learning do not recognize that they are engaged in learning activities because they regard learning primarily as a formal, structured activity that takes place in schools, colleges and universities or on training courses designated for the purpose of acquiring a particular skill (Schuller and Field, 1998).

By contrast, lifelong learning can be perceived as the on-going acquisition of knowledge or skills, based on the idea that learning can, and does, take place beyond the formal structure of an educational institution and occurs throughout a person's lifetime (Field, 2006a). Lifelong learning rather than education became a guiding concept for the continuing education sector in the 1990s (Field, 2003) and embraced a range of ideological positions in educational research, reflecting the conceptual diversity (Ardelt, 2000; Murray, 2011) as well as the multiple approaches and settings attached to 'continuous, personal development' through student-centred (self-actualized) learning (Schuller and Field, 1998: 67).

Social models of lifelong learning

I now turn to consider five social models of lifelong learning, drawn from a range of commentators, which I find particularly helpful. The first of these describes a *deficit model* of lifelong learning. Here, inadequacies in achievements are inappropriately blamed on individual failures rather than on economic and social inequalities (Burke and Jackson, 2007). If individuals blame themselves for past failures in education, they are likely to continue to experience barriers through lack of confidence if they seek to learn later in life. This understanding also separates the social from the individual in the learning process, and encourages learners to accept prescribed knowledge rather than valuing their own experiences or questioning these prescribed definitions. Effectively, control resides in ownership of knowledge (Young, 1971).

The second model, a *social justice model* of lifelong learning, acknowledges a citizen's involvement in the lifelong learning discourse and is defined by Doukas as 'learning through all aspects of life, so that each citizen has the opportunity to acquire the necessary knowledge for personal development, social and professional enhancement, to become an active participant in society and the economy' (Doukas, 2002: 282) and to promote wider access and social justice through such means. This model considers the individual's appreciation of the full and wider benefits of learning and the barriers faced by different groups.

The third model is identified as a *social innovation model* of lifelong learning. Here, Bostrom (2002) describes a model that promotes socio-economic transition and democratization through social stimuli. In this model, lifelong learners are able to develop new thinking by interacting with each other over a period of time, potentially reflecting Freire's (1970) concept of learning for critical consciousness through social engagement. This is best described in the skills- and confidence-based learning that, for example, members of local regeneration boards, such as in the New Deal for Communities, have accessed when working at a local level and being involved in recommending change. Barnes *et al.* (2007) also describe people engaging as more active citizens through learning participation skills in consultative and community-based projects – a model that is also reflected in the 'learning for active citizenship' programmes promoted during the earlier New Labour years. As Mayo and Annette (2010) highlight, there are differences in how such models are played out and some models may serve government agendas through promoting 'good citizens' while others genuinely build greater critical awareness of democratic participation.

Fourthly, lifelong learning can be identified within a *social movement model* (Jarvis, 2007: 42). Such a model recognizes the dynamic and collective outcomes of individuals coming together in shared learning and change activities. For older black women in an ageing society, involvement of this type can be seen where there is a need to address an urgent local social concern. In the context of older black women, it can be said that they are beginning to re-consider a 'lost role, beyond the home' (Etienne and Jackson, 2010: 50), and in such situations learning is considered an integral part of meaningful social participation. The extent to which this social participation extends to become a 'movement' depends on the contexts, stimuli and spaces for action and the resulting collective awareness of participants (Crowther, 2004).

The final social model of lifelong learning I would like to highlight here is described by Griffin (2000) as a *socially progressive movement model*, which differs from the previous models as it seeks to challenge public education systems via a more explicit concept of social and institutional change. In clarifying this definition, Griffin states:

> *If the policy of lifelong learning can be counted ... the question arises as to whether or not it is a socially progressive movement or whether it poses a threat to public education systems and thus to their role in promoting access and equal opportunities.*

(Griffin, 2000: 7)

Outside public education systems, lifelong learning has the potential to provide second and third chances to marginalized learners in the population. Examining these different models, therefore, raises significant questions in relation to the role that lifelong learning can play both in offering access to learning and in empowering older learners.

Women and learning in the community

One of the most striking trends in participation in adult learning is the international phenomenon that, over the last 10–15 years, women have overtaken men in educational achievement at all levels and in almost every subject across most Organisation for Economic Cooperation and Development (OECD) countries (Schuller and Watson, 2009). These authors also found that men are more likely to learn at work or independently, while women are more likely to learn within publicly funded or community facilities. However, minority ethnic women, especially those in older age groups, are not distinguished in the data, which points to the idea that publicly funded and community provision have gender and ethnic implications. The data also have implications for the relationship between gender and age. Women in their forties and above belong to the cohort before the occurrence of dramatic increases in women's levels of qualifications, and are both more in need of, and also less likely to participate in, adult learning (Jones, 2010). There are also a series of barriers that can be identified as hindering older adults from participating in adult learning, ranging from cost, accessibility and information about opportunities, to the appropriateness of provision, in terms of content, pace and cultural relevance of the offer (Jones, 2010).

Increasing educational participation has long been seen as a major factor in achieving greater social equality and in improving wider societal participation (Schuller, 2000). For example, Hills *et al.* (2010: 393) identified that 'low income acts as a barrier to post-compulsory education' and is, in turn, likely to contribute to perpetuating social exclusion. However, in much of this research around social mobility, inclusion and exclusion, older black women are invisible.

Setting the context

This book is located within the wider, largely economic, debates about funding for lifelong learning (NIACE, 2007) and is set against a backdrop of shifting policies and diminishing resources for widening participation and adult learning. Acknowledging the global challenge of an ageing society, it draws on the narratives of groups of older women, exploring the social and political dimensions to lifelong learning, alongside the individual benefits, and questions the extent to which the women's learning also benefits their communities.

As a consequence of migration to Britain from the Caribbean in the 1950s and 1960s, the black Caribbean population aged 65 and over now comprises the largest group of non-white elders in the UK (Dunnell, 2007). For this reason the book focuses on older black women from the Caribbean. However, there are likely to be important similarities in considering lifelong learning across other older black communities in the UK. Many of the women featured in the book arrived in Britain in their early 20s or as young children, and a large number of those interviewed considered themselves 'community activists', volunteering in their local communities and participating in structured learning of one form or another. Often this learning activity is intended to equip them with skills to play a fuller, more active role (Fryer, 2008) in their local neighbourhoods. In some cases those delivering learning activities may design training specifically to develop skills to enable the women to play a more effective role at meetings. In addition, the women themselves may initiate training to help improve their skills in an effort to tackle a particular concern in their community such as social isolation (McCabe *et al.*, 2013). The value of volunteering roles carried out by this group of women is significant in this multi-ethnic society with an increasing number of older citizens.

Why write about an ageing black population?

During the course of my research I was asked by my peers why I had chosen to look at learning and an ageing population (Lievesley, 2010). What was the attraction? More to the point, why study an ageing black population in what is often described as a largely ageist society, far more interested in maximizing the economic potential of the younger and mostly the male population (Maynard, 2002; Annette and Mayo, 2009)? And why specifically the learning needs of an ageing black *female* population? What additional value would an understanding of the motivations of this group bring to the lifelong learning debate? In reply I argued that there were pressing gendered, social, moral (Sutherland, 2006) and economic reasons for studying an ageing black female population, borne out by the large numbers of first-generation African Caribbean women with significant skills acquired from a range of services (Amos and Parmar, 1984; Afshar *et al.*, 2002a), not least from the National Health Service. Learning in later life has been linked to the potential to tackle social exclusion, promote active citizenship (Better Government for Older People, 2000) and – in the context of older women – encourage wellbeing and social participation. For that reason, it seemed irrational, when we are living longer, healthier lives, to ignore older black women's potential contribution to a society where welfare spending is diminishing but the proportional age of the UK population is rising.

I have developed a particular strategy for presenting and interpreting the women's stories in the book and my approach does raise issues about 'voice', representation and interpretive authority (Hertz, 1997). I argue my approach on grounds of my interconnectedness with the women because I am of the same gender, ethnic heritage and social disposition. The acts presented here seek to explain, entertain, inform and challenge (Earthy and Cronin, 2008), and as Chase (2008: 65) describes, also defend and at times confirm the purpose and nature of learning. My reasons for pursuing research with an older black female population emerged from some broad areas of my vocational life that I will now describe briefly.

THE WOMEN'S INSTITUTE EXPERIENCE

When first I worked as a full-time research assistant in higher education it was in an Economic and Social Research Council (ESRC)-sponsored study into lifelong learning and the Women's Institute (WI). I explored how groups of older, white and predominately middle-class women members of the largest voluntary organization for women in the UK interacted with each other in informal learning settings (Etienne and Jackson, 2010). I noted how much the women learned from each other, how they supported each other and how they enjoyed the benefits of informal learning in their later years. Conducting this research gave me valuable insights into the benefits of learning, as perceived by a distinct group of older women learners, and made me aware of the limited research that existed relating to older black women. I learnt from the WI study that being educated and having a high level of social capital can result in better health and happiness for the individual but not necessarily for the wider local community of women.

A good many of the members of the WI involved in the study had already acquired higher education, and informal learning was now playing an important role in maintaining their health and wellbeing. While conducting fieldwork research into the WI in predominantly rural areas of the UK, I noted the total invisibility of older black women in my numerous case study interviews. And although I understood the reasons why older black women were not part of the 'white middle class habitus' (Jackson, 2006) occupied by the WI members, I wondered about the learning lives of black women of my mother's generation.

The black Caribbean population

It was clear that the elderly black population in the UK was growing. When I first embarked on my research among people of colour in the UK, the black Caribbean population had the largest proportion of people aged 65 and over (11 per cent). This reflected the first large-scale migration of non-white groups to Britain in the 1950s, making them the most numerous elderly minority ethnic group (Maynard *et al.*, 2008: 4) in the country. I was interested in the role that older black Caribbean women might play in responding to this change. How might satisfying their educational desires also achieve support for others in an ageing society? Prior to that the National Institute of Adult Continuing Education (NIACE, 2007) had stressed that over the next 50 years the current proportion of black and minority ethnic elders was set to grow significantly.

Older black women learners: Absence from the lifelong learning discourse

I have another reason for my interest in the learning lives of older black women: the absence of black women in the seemingly broad-based lifelong learning literature. Very few academic studies have specifically acknowledged lifelong learning among older black women in the UK. And although studies provided evidence of research into the lives of the older population generally, NIACE underlined that the research on lifelong learning among older black and minority communities remained sparse (NIACE, 2005), while the provision available to them was 'often irrelevant, culturally inappropriate and inaccessible' (NIACE, 2005: 16).

Stella Dadzie's study for NIACE (1993) into educational provision for ethnic minority elders provided an opening for further research in this area but, almost two decades later, there is still little empirical evidence available. In view of the wide acknowledgement of the value of lifelong learning (Field, 2006a; Schuller *et al.*, 2004) and the benefits in particular for older learners (Withnall, 2000; 2003; 2006; Jackson, 2006; Tuckett and McCauley, 2005), why did the literature not include narratives about the first major wave of Caribbean women to enter Britain after the Second World War or, indeed, other black women of my generation?

Volunteering and older black women

The *personal* justification and motivation for my study came from my own volunteering and working life as they gradually came together. First there was my role as a community volunteer with Ujima Housing (until 2008, Britain's oldest and biggest black-led housing association), working with black activists to confront racial discrimination in some of the most ethnically diverse areas of London. In its study of volunteering in the community, the Institute for Volunteering Research (IVR) exposed the link between social exclusion and volunteering and in this context identified volunteering as: 'Offering time and help to others' and involving a 'cost to the volunteer which was greater than any benefit they might receive from the activity' (Paine *et al.*, 2010: 8). From the volunteer's point of view, an earlier study showed that volunteering was considered a mutually beneficial exchange relationship and 'something that provides benefits to the individual, be it enjoyment, skills, or the sense of having given something back' (IVR, 2004: 25). In this context, my research sought to explore the possibilities and extent of such 'mutually beneficial exchange' relationships, largely from the point of view of the women volunteers.

Earlier research into social inequalities and ethnic minorities in Britain (Evandrou, 2000) and more recent studies by the Joseph Rowntree Foundation (2007) revealed high levels of poverty among Britain's black and minority ethnic communities, a fact that is known to erect barriers and prevent access to particular types of learning. Maynard's (2003: 15) research into women from different ethnic and economic backgrounds revealed, however, a growing number of women who were 'more positive and clearly wishing to play an important role in tackling social exclusion and in developing the world around them'. This raises questions for my study about the motivations and benefits of both learning and voluntary action for the women involved and others around them. For older black women, poverty and social exclusion have often blighted their learning aspirations. Cullen *et al.* (2000) noted that informal learning is, in fact, widening participation and that individuals may be able to give back to the wider community by participating in informal community learning.

Teaching in the era of widening participation

As a researcher and social sciences higher education lecturer teaching on widening participation programmes, I worked as an extra-mural and continuing education tutor in higher education in the early 1990s. Here it was not unusual for me to encounter older black women, who volunteered in the community, participating in group tasks on women's access programmes alongside younger learners, developing skills for active citizenship in their local community. My belief then was that their success on these programmes was largely due to their shared cultural backgrounds and the fact that they faced similar struggles in their lives. The women were consequently able to develop strong informal communities of practice (Lave and Wenger, 1991) and it appeared that learning as a form of social and community engagement was highly influential in their lives.

I found the question posed by Mirza when she was conducting research with young people in schools and in higher education relevant. She asked: 'Why, in the context of endemic race and gender inequality, is there a persistent expression of educational desire among black and ethnicised women?' (2009: 8). It seemed that question might be posed equally to older black women activists, and thus it became a key motivation for my fieldwork study. I observed that older black women appeared to have developed greater coping mechanisms to deal with 'endemic race and gender inequality' as a result of their many years of experience of marginalization in both the UK and in the Caribbean. I felt a strong desire to get to the root of these coping mechanisms and to understand their earlier educational experiences and aspirations: what form did these take?

I reflected on my own position, as a tutor and as a researcher of the social world, and considered the involvement of other black women working in similar fields (Phoenix, 1994; Gregory, 2001; Mirza, 2003; Baumgartner and Johnson-Bailey, 2010). What future role might we play in an ageing learning society and how had our educational aspirations been shaped by earlier generations? The narratives in this book convey the essence of conversations occurring in groups and in one-to-one discussions with me where the women participants expressed strong views on their learning and (mis)education, hopes for the future and concerns about issues in the wider black community. The book demonstrates how, in many areas, learning in later years can promote a sense of social responsibility and a purposeful, meaningful life in older age.

The beginning of my own story

I was fascinated with the revelations of the early learning experiences of the first-generation African Caribbean women I interviewed. As a second-generation African Caribbean woman whose own parents came to the UK from St Lucia in the late 1950s, I could see enormous similarities in the women's stories. But I also acknowledged huge disparities, which left me questioning the nature of past and present inequality as it affected older black women learners in the UK. My story in the British education system began at Rokesley infant and junior school in Hornsey, North London, where as a child I experienced some bittersweet moments fraught with contradictions, and occasional but painful bullying from pupils who blighted my learning but served to sharpen my learning trajectory. As a black working-class child with a father working on the assembly line at Ford's car manufacturing factory and a devoted but extremely driven mother who worked as a hospital auxiliary nurse, I always knew they had high expectations of my education.

At a very early age I took on responsibility for the chores in the home while looking after my four brothers. An incident that will always remain with me occurred in the almost all-white middle-class primary school I attended. One fateful day, the smartly dressed Mr Law roared loudly at me for being late for school lunch and I stood petrified as he publicly scolded me. It was like a scene from his highly animated reading of *The Lion, the Witch and the Wardrobe*. Like a drill sergeant, he ordered me to stand up straight in the school dining hall and demanded an explanation. I stood in terrified silence for what seemed like an eternity while the other pupils ate and sniggered at my plight. The public humiliation was unbearable as I contemplated the consequences. My year teacher went on to describe me to my parents as being 'disengaged', which my mother only understood as 'disobedient'. On the day she was told, I received a severe reprimand from her about 'playing with my education' and my 'responsibility to the family'.

And so very early on in my education, I was labelled a 'disengaged' learner and by the end of the first term in secondary school my head teacher was telling my parents: 'She is aloof and will need to expand her vocabulary if she is to find her way.' The school advised my parents that I would have to make a real effort to mix with the other pupils if I was to achieve any real progress. This comment from the school was the final straw in a series of disappointments for my mother because, for her, I was now officially a problem in secondary school. It was painful for her but my worsening terror of making mistakes further weakened my ability to socialize with my peers. I had moved to the prestigious Hornsey High School for girls, a former grammar school – now a new comprehensive – and became overwhelmed with anxiety. At the opening of the new school on Inderwick Road, the existing teachers were greeted by a large number of black pupils, including myself, wearing an array of misplaced uniforms as we awaited the arrival of our orders from Keevans, the local school uniform suppliers.

The newly re-named Hornsey School for Girls had lost its grammar school status and I was placed at the bottom of the class, in the lowest stream where the majority of black pupils ended up. This was no surprise to me because I was, after all, already identified at primary level as having difficulties. I can recall what I now might perhaps understand as some disappointment on the faces of the long-serving grammar school teachers. They were clearly sorely missing their former pupils who had passed the 11+ examination and they now had the privilege of teaching us underperforming learners.

One rare source of excitement was the fact that as new pupils we were allowed to continue using the luxurious black report folders with the regal 'Hornsey High School' crest inscribed in gold on the front cover. The folders impressed me greatly as each term our handwritten school reports were neatly placed inside. In my first report to my parents, the headteacher told them that despite my poor vocabulary she would 'ensure that I was given much realisation and hope'. I believe this may have manifested itself in my appropriately categorized class known as '1AZ'. However, despite the 'A' in the middle everyone at the school knew that the group was in fact '1Z'. This label affected me emotionally and I was so embarrassed by my form classification that after leaving school I tore off the '1AZ' from the bottom of the report page so that no one else could acknowledge my original secondary school class status.

Image and text courtesy of Linda Dujon

Figure 1: Frances and family – New arrivals seeking housing

Introducing the chapters that follow

In the chapters that follow I present the narrative reality (Gubrium and Holstein, 2001) prevalent in the stories told by first-generation African Caribbean women learning in informal settings in the community. It was in these setting that I first wondered about the powerful nature of informal learning occurring in social networks and began to re-consider the question posited by Lave and Wenger (1991: 14): 'What kinds of social engagements provide the proper context for learning to take place?' The stories I present are primarily from group interviews about how older black women learn alongside each other. In interviews, the women spoke sternly to each other in Caribbean patois and constantly challenged each other. Although they were joking with each other, their narratives are profound and display the nuances of their lived experiences from a variety of Caribbean islands.

The chapters reveal how older black women pass on learning strategies in 'womanist ways' (Walker, 1983; Eaton, 2007) through their conversations, and how they constantly discover new confidences through provoking and challenging one another. They show how shared and individual cultural identities present themselves and how the women relate to each other using Caribbean expressions passed on through the generations. I was bombarded with the familiar Caribbean greetings, expressions and cultural accusations such as: 'sakafet', 'playing mas', 'labrish', 'hickass', 'mamaguise', 'commess', 'margee', 'salop', 'bobolos', 'malpop' and 'vesearse'.

In this book, such terminologies form part of the women's identity and their African heritage. Creole patois, a combination of the regional African language and the language of the slave master (English, French, Dutch or other) is spoken by many of the women who were born on the colonized islands and whose great-grandparents directly experienced the atrocities of slavery. Their West Indian dialects and expressions vary from island to island depending on their particular colonial influence. In this book, many of the expressions and greetings used by the women in their interactions with each other have roots in the French colonized Eastern Caribbean islands where a form of French Creole language (Frank, 2001) is still commonly spoken.

The acts and scenes

My interactions with the women and their learning environments are captured in a series of stories, employing dramatic acts and scenes to depict the various elements and plot lines in the narratives and the settings in which they are told. Narrative reality (Riessman, 2001) refers to the socially situated practice of storytelling, implying that the contexts in which the women tell their stories are as much a part of this reality as the words recorded in my transcripts. Drawing on my fieldwork notes I was able to recapture such narrative realities, in particular locations and settings, as I exposed the nuances in the stories. At the beginning of each act, I set the scene using italics like in a dramatic script, by sketching a picture of the locality where the interviews took place to situate the participants. I offer insight into the particular learning contexts or projects (such as learning in a community housing, city challenge regeneration area) with a title such as 'Learning for challenge'. The background of the participants often emerges in the form of a critical narrative delivered by a woman in the study. I also use italics for short asides that indicate a particular point of action or occurrence.

I position myself inside the text and interject to make key points with dramatized annotations. These comments are made by the Narrator character and are intended as asides spoken to the audience and not heard by others within the narrative. Thus I can interrogate issues and demonstrate the nature of learning as the woman tells her story. I have immersed myself in the stories as someone who has acquired knowledge from the range of interviews with Caribbean women in their homes or within their projects plus understandings of critical issues in the storylines imbued with my second-generation African Caribbean identity. While the stories depict critical themes such as humiliation, shame and poverty, the conversations were laced with laughter and expressions of happiness as the women described how they tackled adversity in their learning lives.

All acts in the following chapters reveal the nature of the polyrhythmic realities prevalent in the interactions of first-generation African Caribbean women participating in the study. This is how the older black Caribbean women express their multiple and varied voices. Many of the stories reveal frustrations in learning, conflicts and struggles but also fond memories of happier times, of hopes. And they invariably reveal plotlines that highlight both the significance of, and barriers to, learning in the women's lives.

Preserving authenticity in the women's narratives

The women I interviewed regularly spoke to me, and to each other, using the present tense when mainstream grammar would use past tenses. Their stories were littered with such 'differently' presented tenses as 'She try so hard' instead of 'She tried so hard'; and 'She send him to the auntie', meaning 'She sent him to the auntie'. Despite my heritage, other aspects of language and particular enunciations sometimes challenged me. But to preserve the authenticity of the stories and capture the character and characteristics of the speakers, I have chosen not to correct the women's vocabulary or grammar since they depict a different reality and capture the diversity and nuances of language from across the Caribbean islands. However, at times, I have used my role as narrator to make meanings clearer to a wider readership and I have used the dramatic present tense in introducing the acts and scenes.

While engaging with black womanism (for example, Collins, 2000a; Hudson-Weems, 2004), the book exposes the intersectional relationships evident in the social settings where learning takes place. The women's narratives highlight past, current and future educational dilemmas as they interact across age, Caribbean island and social class divides. I seek to display the women's experiencing of education and learning (Alfred, 2004), showcasing their learning histories and the barriers they face in accessing learning. Ultimately I want to extend the spaces in literature where the hitherto absent voices of older black women can be represented.

Throughout the time I was constructing the study, I considered my own womanist determination to improve the lives of women and to be part of the dialogue for change. I became acutely aware of my own desire for higher levels of education, both to help myself and also to empower other black women to develop individually and collectively and extend the boundaries of study. This mutual aspiration for higher learning and education as a 'good' that is invulnerable is captured in a poem by Caribbean poet Louise Bennett:

> *Mi full up mi purse wid money,*
> *Dem tief it weh from me.*
> *Mi full up mi belly wid food*
> *An as mi sneeze mi feel hungry.*
> *Mi full up mi brain wid learnin,*
> *Wid sense and Knowledge gran,*
> *Mi feel relief not a tief can tief*
> *Mi education!*
>
> (Extract 1 from a poem entitled *Education*.
> Bennett, 1982: 12)

Being part of a wider community of learning at any age is of significant value. And for older black women, who face potentially higher levels of marginalization, learning in later life is likely to have significant benefits. This book throws light on an important but neglected area of learning and the people who pursue it.

Chapter 2

Lifelong learning in womanist ways

In the space of 15 months I interviewed 103 women in groups and one-to-one. The interviews were conducted in locations including community centres, African Caribbean heritage centres, social clubs, community halls, tenants' halls, local colleges, church halls and women's homes. Their ages ranged from 52 to 101. Although I acknowledge the struggles of black men and boys in UK society, I focused solely on the narratives of older black women – a decision that, at times, created a dilemma, as we will see.

ACT 1: A story of reading inside matriarchal learning hubs

CAST OF CHARACTERS*

NARRATOR	The INTERVIEWER speaks to the audience, as an aside
INTERVIEWER	Speaks directly to the characters
ELCINA	Aged 52, from Grenada
TILLEY	Aged 72, from Jamaica
ANSELMA	Aged 71, from St Lucia
PAMELA	Aged 65, from Jamaica
PATRICIA	Aged 68, from Barbados
MARY	Aged 70, from St Kitts

*Throughout all the acts, pseudonyms are used and interview locations are fictitious.

SCENE 1: *Approaching the learning environment*

Twilight sets on a seemingly quiet residential street in the heart of multicultural Meads, and as the INTERVIEWER walks alongside a stylish row of social housing she makes her way toward the 'Staying for Now' Project. Standing at the front door, she hears intense laughter and the shouts of West Indian women engaged in lively banter. She could detect the variations in the Caribbean dialects, from the Bajan shrill, to the curt Jamaican patois and then to the deep Kittitian 'swagger'. She marvels at what she considers an unusual mixing of Caribbean women in an informal social setting in the North of England. The youngest woman in the group (ELCINA) moves hurriedly to greet the interviewer at the door.

ELCINA: *(still laughing, speaks in an unexpected Yorkshire accent)* They're a bit lively today. *(draws the INTERVIEWER into the small hall)* Yes, they're all preparing for Black History Month. Take a look at this. *(the INTERVIEWER moves forward and peers closely at the colourful table)* Just look at this display *(she whispers)*. A blast from the past, don't you think?

NARRATOR: I could only describe what I saw as forbidden treasures that could have been lifted from my mother's front room: the hatbox containing the white faded church hat; the familiar array of bright plastic flowers; the large, blue glass fish ornament; and the tall painting of the light-skinned, near naked, black woman with her very long black hair draped across one side of her body. All these sacred items no doubt represented apparently happier times for my mother and the women I was about to be introduced to.

ELCINA: I am learning so much about the stories behind these memorabilia.

The INTERVIEWER draws closer to the display and gazes at the subject of the intense laughter: an old black and white photograph of an elegantly dressed lady. One woman (TILLEY) holds this prized possession in her hands.

TILLEY: Sister Agnes made that dress for the wedding but when the man never show up we had it fix up for the Lyceum ballroom! *(louder laughter)*

NARRATOR: The woman in the photograph was wearing a white dress with a small white knitted cardigan. Her smooth pressed hair was worn in sharp outward curls. She sat on a sofa, her light stockings contrasting with her black pointed-toe shoes. She had one open hand positioned on an open book, which was strategically placed on her lap. Her other hand was clutching a half-filled champagne glass that was pressed against her face.

SCENE 2: *Memories of the front line*

TILLEY: Pure water ina dat glass! *(more laughter)*

TILLEY: *(mischievously shouting above the laugher)* But tell me, what you ah read there Ms Anselma?

There is suddenly a moment of stillness and silence in the room. Laughter ceases. The noisy, frivolous scene comes to an abrupt end as the interviewer approaches the women.

PAMELA: (*speaking in a curt and unfriendly tone*) If you come here to talk 'bout slavery – don't bother cum here wid dat!

INTERVIEWER: (*appearing visibly uncomfortable at hearing this sharp statement*) No, the research concerns ... (*trails off when the laughter immediately returns and the interviewer is ignored as the women resume their random conversations*)

MARY: She used to be pretty you know! (*laugher from all*)

TILLEY: If you see walk she did ah walk ina dem same shoes.

PATRICIA: But you no easy Miss Anselma. (*PATRICIA stares at ANSELMA mockingly, and is laughing at her own statement*)

ANSELMA: You salop. You like ro-ro too much!

TILLEY: But you is me long time friend and dem days was good times ... 'member when ... (*the women are laughing incessantly*)

NARRATOR: Tilley was in upbeat mode about the memories she was sharing with the women about her antics at the blues dances alongside her long-time friend Anselma, always by her side, and today sitting next to her as they prepared their images for the 'Liming on the Frontline' oral history project. They were about to share their stories of informal learning with me.

ELCINA: Okay, let us give the interviewer some time now.

NARRATOR: Appearing to be rude was just par for the course among the older black women. Though not altogether surprised, as my research interviews will demonstrate, I was often tested out by the women.

SCENE 3: *Emphasizing ethnic heritage*

INTERVIEWER: So my research project is entitled 'First-generation African Caribbean Women' and ... (*experiencing a further uncomfortable moment, interrupted by MARY*)

MARY: Pardon me?

NARRATOR: At once it was clear that the women had a major concern, not only about the nature of the research but also about how they would be referred to.

PAMELA: (*sharply, with loud support from the other women*) Now stop there child! Wat dis African? Listen here. We are West Indians!

ANSELMA: But of course we are not African. We are West Indians!

ELCINA: But there are women from Africa who also volunteer here at the centre (*the assertion appears to be made to support the researcher*).

MARY: Yes, but we are not Africans?

ELCINA: Africans and Caribbeans work well together here at this project.

ANSELMA: Ler me tell you child. You not listening Elcina. We are West Indians! (*'Not Africans' is repeated by the other women*)

PATRICIA: Not African thank you very much!

The interviewer does not seek to challenge but acquiesces and politely moves on to ask the women about the nature of their learning projects:

INTERVIEWER: Thank you. How you wish to be represented is very important to me.

TILLEY: Don't bother try test us.

ANSELMA: Hickass! Vesearse! (*provoking laughter from the women as the INTERVIEWER tries not to look embarrassed*)

SCENE 4: *Learning activities*

TILLEY: I think the 'Staying for Now' project is good because it keeps our minds alive. We can remember tings together and if we were not together we would not remember.

PATRICIA: Anselma can remind us how to look up things on the Internet and how to open up a document. She is very good at that. But I come here once a month for the carnival committee meetings – I don't get involved in all that jump up (laugh) and playing mas nonsense, but they like to get us oldies involved because we are original West Indians.

The INTERVIEWER is told more about the work of the project and how the women were involved with others in their community.

MARY: They watched some of the film about the great British black invasion and I talked to them about my experience and Anselma chat bout Anancy stories and the photographs that they had put up on display.

PATRICIA: Lots of things we did not know before because they show the film in sections and every time there is something new. I do like going out and doing these things because it makes me forget my diabetes. You can get scared if you spend time thinking too much about that. (*she laughs at her statement*)

ANSELMA: Let me tell you eh – the pleasure of working together with other West Indian women who are not afraid to speak their minds is a powerful thing for me. I feel very good about having this opportunity to express myself how I want to and not to feel shy about it.

MARY: I feel very liberated.

ANSELMA: I get some good feedback – and they are not always good (*laughs*) – mostly bad from her! (*laughing again, louder, and looking at TILLEY*)

MARY: I know that life in this country was hard at first for all of us and in some ways it is still hard but we have stuck together and have shared many things together and it's nice that we can really do rewarding things now. We learn a lot from each other. I feel a sense of purpose when I am with the other women and enjoy what I do even though it is very hard work just having to come here sometimes. (*all the women are laughing*)

Image and text courtesy of Cleo Shillingford

Figure 2: Neola and Cleo – New arrivals on their first day of seeking employment

TILLEY: And if we lose this centre I don't know what we will do? The council trowing people out left, right and centre.

ELCINA: They cannot afford these centres. Everything nowadays needs to make money.

NARRATOR: As the discussion developed, the importance of the group and the shared dialogue and experiences started to emerge, alongside both more concrete learning experiences and personal motivations. In response to my questions, I heard about the women's reasons for attending, alongside insights into their personal lives. I also learnt about their attitudes to the behaviour of young students they came into contact with while volunteering.

TILLEY: They don't misbehave at the university, not like at the college where they have their feet on the chairs and the teachers don't say a damn ting.

PATRICIA: The youngsters have no respect for us. They are ungrateful and deserve to experience the education system back home. When they get bad like that, the whole lot of dem should be shipped back to get a taste of the licks in the West Indies.

ANSELMA: But things are not the same in the West Indies anymore.

PAMELA: They are the same alright.

PATRICIA: They have no manners at the college and I give dem a mouthful when I does get a chance. At the university the young students have manners. I like dat. Good manners.

ANSELMA: Not like you. (*all laughing*) Malpop.

ELCINA: But they have manners at the school too.

TILLEY: Yes, until they get into the gangs.

SCENE 5: Anselma's story

NARRATOR: In my one-to-one interview with Anselma, who was the subject in the photograph and the key reason for the excitement in Scene 2, I uncovered feelings of sadness, frustration and shame but also of pride, determination and hope.

ANSELMA: I brought along my book today, *Sense and Sensibility,* that I had since I was young.

INTERVIEWER: Why is this book so important to you?

ANSELMA: Let me tell you – this was really and truly the start of my learning.

INTERVIEWER: What parts of the book did you find most interesting?

ANSELMA: You don't know how that book did make me feel.

NARRATOR: I wanted to find out more about Anselma's possible learning from the book and what it meant to her but initially the responses I had hoped to gain were not forthcoming.

INTERVIEWER: Back then, what was in the book that made you treasure it so much?

ANSELMA: That book really helped me a lot.

NARRATOR: Anselma had either not understood my question or she was deliberately not acknowledging my need to know. I considered my question and its possible judgemental leaning. Was it that I was more interested in why this book would be of interest to an older black Caribbean woman? I was convinced that it would not have interested my mother, who was of a similar age and heritage. However, the plotline suddenly emerged and I finally realized that Anselma had understood perfectly what was meant by my question. Visibly weighing up how far to trust me, she closed her eyes for a few seconds.

ANSELMA: I had this book but I could not read it back then; I did not know how to read.

The INTERVIEWER appears uncomfortable that she had not understood the reasons for ANSELMA's initial reticence earlier.

ANSELMA: Yes, the book was really of no use to me back then. But I always knew I would be able to read it one day.

NARRATOR: Suddenly I realized the curious and fulfilling role that the Staying for Now project was playing. It had taken Anselma a long time before she eventually shared with the other volunteers at the project her lack of confidence in reading. Once she was able to do this, she progressed swiftly. The strap-line in the project's leaflet read: 'Reading is useful; take your turn to read together for pleasure at the "Staying for Now" project'.

ANSELMA: But now I have been slowly reading it and I get to read aloud as well. (*laughs*) And don't mind the others – they like to hear my voice (*chuckling*). In our group, although the women are loud, we are very private. We have confidences and we trust each other.

SCENE 6: *Anselma's story: Humiliation in the classroom*

ANSELMA: Nowadays I want to learn as much as I can. I come to the project to read and write with others and to get some more computer skills. When I was back home growing up I was poor and when you were that poor you did not go to school much and when you did, you was always late, because you was forever working in the yard. Sometime my grandfather would say 'It's time for school to finish' as he wanted me in the house to have his food on the table.

The teachers back home – they well and truly ruled. They could say anything to you and get away with it. If they were not serious they would be sarcastic with you and you could not even answer back (not that you would). I really suffered with one named Teacher Belcher who for no reason was so facety to me. That day when he asked me to stand up in front of the class and spell the word 'black' – I remember it so well. At the time I was thinking, why is he asking me that? I could not really see the point then. He already did know that I could not read. I felt so humiliated. All the other children were laughing at me. This was on account that I was very black and very ugly. I hated going to school to be humiliated in that way. He just used to like making fun of me and it was very hurtful. I just stopped trying from then.

NARRATOR: Discrimination on the basis of skin colour (Gabriel, 2007) has for some time been recognized as an issue in the Caribbean. Some might say that lighter-skinned people in the Caribbean once had more social capital and enjoyed positions of power in a whole range of areas, particularly in politics. In Anselma's case, her teacher (Mr Belcher), a light-skinned black man, employed this form of colour victimization. It was treated as a joke but it hurt and de-motivated Anselma, making her unwilling to learn to read. This affected her lifelong education and learning.

I went back to my transcript of the group interview to appreciate how Anselma's past experiences were impacting on her interactions with others in the project.

SCENE 7: *Reading and learning*

A group interview is taking place.

INTERVIEWER: What was the book you were reading over and over again?

ANSELMA: *Sense and Sensibility.* My aunt who was a teacher at the convent gave it to me before she died. She was ill for a long time and I felt so good when she gave me that book. I brought the book to England with me and I have kept it ever since. Because she always called me her young lady – now I know why. I like reading about the English ways ... I enjoyed reading all the good things ... the different life ... it was like a fairytale to me. I still think of English people like that sometimes ... the real English people ... You know everyone with manners and everything – but not anymore – I see all sorts of English people now! (*laughing*)

INTERVIEWER: What did you learn from reading the book?

TILLEY: She never read the book. Only now she ah read the book!

ANSELMA: Let me tell you. Yes I can now read the book. I took it to the first writers' meeting because they asked us to bring something that was important to us. At one time I would say other people's treasures was koshoni and other people (*looking at Tilley*) might say that this was margee but it is special to me. Yes it is true I could not read it before but I get better after each paragraph.

TILLEY: See what I telling you!

INTERVIEWER: So Anselma, what did you learn from the book?

ANSELMA: About the upper class, posh people and the posh way they speak and the things they say that sound good. Like: 'She was sensible and clever, but eager in everything, her sorrows, her joys could have no moderation'.

PAMELA: Here we go.

PATRICIA: You want to see the book. She wrap it up so nice, like a treasure, but the book was so old. She fill her head with pure nonsense. Wake up Anselma! You are in the twenty-first century!

ANSELMA: Yes you can call it margee – but what you reading? Having that book was good for my learning but you see how these malpops (*pointing at the women*) gave me a hard time.

INTERVIEWER: What was it about that book that made you hold on to it for so long?

ANSELMA: Not you as well. (*the women are laughing*)

ANSELMA: I just knew that as long as I had it I would be important – when I was young. Everyone saw me as somebody. It made me think I was clever – even though I was not! (*laughing*)

Review of Act 1

This act revealed certain boundaries – related to what the women were not prepared to discuss and how they wished to be known – that they guarded vehemently. Scene 3 revealed the women's rejection of the term 'African Caribbean' in favour of 'West Indian'. In Scene 4 they provided insights into the nature of activities within the project, while in Scene 5 one woman introduces the importance in her life of a particular book. In Scene 6 the same woman describes her early experiences of humiliation in the classroom; and, finally, in Scene 7, the significance of the book that was the focus of attention in Scene 2 is exposed as a source of strength in overcoming an inability to read in adult life. The act provides initial insights into polyrhythmic reality at play in the sisterly banter evident in the women's interactions.

Exploring black feminist thought

I now turn to a particular line of exploration drawing on black feminist approaches in the works of Collins (2000a), Hudson-Weems (2004) and Sheared (1999). My thoughts are also informed by the work of hooks (1989), Bennett (1982), Barriteau (2004), Reynolds (2005), Mirza (2009), Abrams (2010) and others. In drawing inferences from the principles of black feminist thought, paying close attention to the common principles of community, culture, oral tradition and the voice of black women, I note the connectedness with the stories I engage with in my study. While observing how the women in Act 1 interacted with each other and with me, I was informed by a type of Africentric feminist epistemology, a perspective that emphasizes the intersection of multiple, polyrhythmic realities or the multiple polyrhythmic realities that flow through one's being (Sheared, 1999). Such polyrhythmic realities can be seen in the additional stories of informal learning that follow.

Sheared developed a model that represents such intersecting polyrhythmic realities based on the Africentric feminist deconstruction of an individual's worldview (Sheared, 1996). The work of Sheared re-asserted four assumptions from her viewpoint as a framework for giving voice to black learners. I have drawn on these assumptions to relate to older black women's experiences of the concept of caring for the wider community and the nature of personal accountability in particular. While the key focus of my research is on those first-generation African Caribbean women who came to Britain in the 1950s and early 1960s, I was mindful that black people have been present in the UK for centuries: the first wave connected with slavery and the second with empire (Jaggi, 2000). Therefore the knowledge expressed by women participating in the study would not only reflect their own lived experiences but also the shared memories gained from interacting with others.

Carby (1997: 49) acknowledges that post-war British 'wives and mothers were granted entry into paid work only so long as this did not harm the family'. Yet women from Britain's reserve army of labour in the colonies were recruited into the labour force far beyond any such considerations. Ellis (1985) highlights the responsibility of researchers not only to give voice to those who may be oppressed or absent from research but also to share the wider critical understanding, noting:

> *If education is to have any real value for women it must not only raise their consciousness about the oppressive structures that keep them in positions of powerlessness, it must also help them to understand the nature of the social, economic and political systems in which they operate and which operate against them.*
>
> (Ellis, 1985: 100)

I set out to explore the value and benefits of lifelong learning for groups of older learners who are motivated to learn and work with others in the community but who are often low in the socio-economic order. However, while I have argued that the research process can extend insights, as Ellis (1985) identifies, it is important to consider also the social responsibilities and moral principles that acknowledge subjects' empowerment and challenge paradigms that sustain existing inequalities.

Black women, learning and a sense of community

Black women have experienced multiple levels of discrimination and many have sacrificed a large part of their younger years to support others. Why should learning matter at this late stage in their lives? How useful might it be to the women themselves or to society? I found some answers in exploring the notion of community, which in the context of first-generation African Caribbean women can best be understood by acknowledging a collective struggle to combat discrimination at the hands of a new and uncertain society (Amos and Parmar, 1984; Bryan *et al.*, 1985; Mirza, 2003). Across the African diaspora, black women have, for some time now, sought a distinct voice to declare their determination to serve the community. As Alice Walker (1982: 21) points out in *The Color Purple*, 'So, we teach the young ones, babysit the babies, look after the old and sick, and attend birthing mothers. Our days are fuller than ever.' This depiction of social or community responsibility is demonstrated in a variety of other ways: in giving priority to education and self-determination (Cooper, quoted in May, 2007); in finding our voice through womanist prose and speeches (Angelou, 1978; Walker, 1983; Lorde, 1984); in developing black feminist thought (Collins, 1990); and in challenging each other through Africana womanism (Hudson-Weems, 2004; Ntiri, 2001; Dove, 1998).

The need for women in the black community to self-identify outside traditional white feminist labels and promote a distinct discourse for the community of black women has been stridently defended (hooks, 2001; Hudson-Weems, 1998). hooks, in particular, points to the position of the black woman in society and the special bond between us, and asserts that she had 'not known a life where women had not been together, where women had not helped, protected and loved one another deeply' (hooks, 2001: 37). Community linked with cultural identity thus resonates strongly despite its multiple meanings and ambiguities. Yet, across the African diaspora and from black feminists in the Caribbean (Andaiye, 2002; Bailey and Leo-Rhynie, 2004) in particular, there is also acknowledgement of the need for critical voices to be heard. However, Caribbean feminist Barriteau identifies a collective deficit when she asks: 'Why haven't Caribbean feminists consciously utilised the theoretical tools of black feminist scholarship? How much do we know about these theoretical contributions?' (Barriteau, 2007: 10).

If Caribbean women acknowledge this as a deficit in their knowledge and as a form of oppression, they will also see that being oppressed means the absence of choices (Bhavnani, 2001: 34). hooks, therefore, encourages us to find our own voices and critically reflect and analyse our place in society because, as black women, our role in the community, and therefore our collective potential, is strong. Gregory showed how black faculty women in American academies are more likely than other groups to be 'overburdened with outside responsibilities to the community' (Gregory, 2001: 125). However, Amos and Parmar (1984) warn us that although it is important to draw on the theory and experiences of black women in the US *and elsewhere* where significant debate has emerged, black women in Britain need to locate their experiences within the context of what is happening in their own lives.

Black British feminism: Learning, community and class

Black British feminism (Mirza, 1997) also places community at the centre of its theoretical frame. In her study of black Caribbean mothers in the UK, Reynolds notes: 'To date African-American feminists' perspectives have dominated the theorisation of black women's experiences and the production of a black woman's knowledge' (2005: 21). She has called for a UK-based black feminist standpoint theory (Reynolds, 2002) that seeks to position black women at the centre instead of the margins of debate so that they might assume an active role in (re)naming and (re)defining their own lives. Like Collins, Reynolds believes that at the heart of black feminist standpoint theory is the view that there exists a 'specialised knowledge produced by black women that clarifies a particular standpoint of and about black women' (Reynolds, 2002: 596) and that these (potentially multiple) standpoints need better dissemination.

As a black British womanist researcher of Caribbean heritage, I seek to uncover such specialized knowledge in the older African Caribbean community to enable older black women to be included in the lifelong learning debate. This shared platform of emerging knowledge comes in many forms, and reflects desires from the earlier struggles (Jones, 1952; Parmar, 1990; Bhavnani, 2001) of black African Caribbean mothers, as depicted by Caribbean poet Jean Binta Breeze expressing the desire to escape from a mundane life:

> Ordinary Mawning
> *it wasn't no duppy frighten mi*
> *mek mi jump outa mi sleep*
> *eena bad mood*
> *nor no neighbour bring first quarrel*
> *to mi door*
> *wasn't de price rise pon bus fare*
> *an milk an sugar*
> *wasjusanadda*
> *same way mawning*
> *anadda clean up de mess*
> *after demlefmawning*
> *a perfectly ordinary*
> *mawning of a perfectly*
> *ordinary day*
> *trying to see a way*
> *out*

(Binta Breeze, 1988: 7)

In their study of black women's lives in Britain, Bryan *et al.* offer another standpoint that reflects on historical experiences and aspirations. They point to the roots of such desires for a way out, noting:

> *Education has always been a burning issue for Black women and viewed in the aftermath of slavery, as virtually the only means for us, and our children to escape the burden of poverty and exploitation, it was regarded in the Caribbean as a kind of liberation.*
>
> (Bryan *et al.*, 1985: 59)

Similarly, Reynolds suggests, in her study of mothering, that learning for black women cannot be understood in isolation from the intersections of race, class, gender and community: 'The development of the concept of "community mothering" reveals first, the social and collective responsibility Caribbean mothers have for children (and other vulnerable members) in their local community, to whom they are not biologically or legally related' (Reynolds, 2005: 120).

Although both studies focus on the interconnected nature of education, socio-economic and female emancipation, Reynolds stresses the social and communal endeavours that enable interdependent learning, offering insight into the significance of collective educational aspirations.

While black feminist standpoint theory has highlighted the importance of understanding both a distinctive British perspective and of placing black women at the centre of debates, the work of authors such as Reynolds has also drawn criticism of their theoretical position. For example, in a previous study, Sudbury argued that black feminist standpoint theory promoted divisiveness because it appeared to ascribe superiority of knowledge or insight on the basis of the scale of oppression. Therefore: '"dark skinned" women could claim to be better judges of racism than "light skinned" black women: heterosexual women could be silenced in the light of lesbian women's assumed insight' (Sudbury, 1998: 29).

These earlier challenges to black feminist standpoint theory in the UK persist and are echoed in contemporary political debates (Taylor *et al.*, 2009). They indicate the nature of discussions that might emerge inside older black women's informal learning spaces, involving both first- and second-generation African Caribbean women.

Returning to Act 1 while reflecting on Anselma's story, I realized how important it was to have allowed her the opportunity to present her thoughts in her own time and at her own pace, enabling the mystery behind her story to unfold. I was then able to uncover a number of perspectives that revealed the full significance of the treasured book. Such different perspectives included status, aspiration, hope, joy and pride. The status in possessing the book, despite being unable to read it, was important to

Anselma as it signified aspiration. The joy and hope were clearly evident in the pose for an important photograph (Scenes 1 and 2) taken soon after her arrival in the UK, where the same open book took pride of place. The title and content of the book represented pride in their association with England and Englishness. But all this was perhaps far from the inaccessible learning culture Anselma had encountered before she acquired greater confidence due to the *Staying for Now* project.

Conclusion

In outlining a theoretical framework drawn from black feminist epistemologies, I consider the tensions between black American feminist perspectives and black British feminist standpoints over several decades. American scholars have significantly developed thinking in this field, including ideas around shared voice and polyrhythmic realities, to which I will return later. However, for this book, it is important to locate black feminist thought firmly in a UK setting to explore and extend insights around a distinct black British womanism, rich in educational desires and with a collective community-focused mission.

The stories told in these chapters suggest there is an important feminist perspective to be heard. And not only feminism but also the interwoven nature or intersectionality of a variety of cultural perspectives appears critical. As Sheared's (1999) study into 'giving voice to learners' lived experiences' highlights, researchers need to recognize the multiple cultural needs of black women learners, in particular the variety of social and community settings in which they are actively involved. Women of my mother's generation are proud women and I turn again to the words of Caribbean poet Ms Lou (Louise Bennett) for her constant reminder of the shame to be expected for not pursuing education in the motherland:

> *Mas Joseph tun-foot nephew,*
> *Jane twis-mout gal Ritty,*
> *Tata daughter a study fi University.*
> *Dem countenance not handsome,*
> *Dem station is not gran',*
> *Dem clothes a wreck*
> *but dem brains can tek education.*
> *Education, education, education,*
> *If yu bright den yuh got de right – to Education!*
> (Extract from poem entitled *Education*.
> Bennett, 1982: 12)

Chapter 3

Speaking up for sisters

Narrative study or narrative inquiry is an interdisciplinary study of the activities involved in generating and analysing data of life experiences. It seeks to understand how people make meaning in their lives. The research becomes a collaborative endeavour – a mutually constructed story from both researcher and participants (Connelly and Clandinin, 1999). This type of research study is concerned with storytelling and is not just about focusing on the content that participants communicate (Hollingsworth and Dybdahl, 2007) but also about the social interactions between interviewer and interviewee (audience and narrator). As a result of the narrative turn, research broadly adopting this approach has been used in a range of different disciplines. In this chapter, I engage with the sociological dimensions (storytelling), drawing on the work of Denzin (1989b), Holstein and Gubrium (1998), Bell (2002), Riessman (2002), Connelly and Clandinin (2006) and Chase (2008), in particular.

I chose contemporary narrative study because it allowed me to involve a wider range of participants across diverse locations in the fieldwork and to locate my own experience and background at every stage of the process. Narrative study comprises 'an amalgam of interdisciplinary analytic lenses, diverse disciplinary approaches, and both traditional and innovative methods – all revolving around an interest in biographical particulars as narrated by the one who lives them' (Chase, 2008: 58). Rather than immerse myself fully in ethnographic fieldwork, this approach enabled a greater focus on narrative construction from a variety of perspectives (Franzosi, 1998; Bell, 2002; Riessman, 2002; Chase, 2008). It enabled me to explore phenomena that emerged from learning through narratives and the detail of the social worlds (Gillham, 2005: 8) projected in the minds of the participants.

ACT 2: Speaking-up for community:
A story of conversation

CAST OF CHARACTERS

NARRATOR The INTERVIEWER speaks to the audience, as an aside

INTERVIEWER Speaks directly to the characters

EDITH	Aged 64, from St Kitts; volunteer worker, (disabled) coordinator of Elders Talk: Oral history project
ROSAMOND	Aged 74, from St Lucia; volunteer at Elders Talk; awarded a community champion award by the local council; mother of Jonetta
JONETTA	Aged 53, from St Lucia; Elders Talk Project worker, organizer of the learning project
SHIRLEY	Aged 71, from St Lucia; member of Elders Talk
MINNIE	Aged 54, from Jamaica; cook at Elders Talk luncheon club; mother of Horatio
CINDY	Aged 61, from St Vincent; serves the tea at Elders Talk
MAUD	Aged 68, from Guyana
ROSA	Aged 67, from Trinidad
SYLVIA	Aged 72, from Barbados
DELL	Aged 66, from Jamaica
CYNTHIA	Aged 52, from Dominica
LILLY	Aged 80, from Montserrat
MILDRED	Aged 80, from Dominica
JUNE	Aged 55, from Jamaica
MARLENE	Aged 69, from Antigua

SCENE 1: Approaching the informal learning centre

A little way out of the underground station the INTERVIEWER can hear familiar cries from a despairing voice: 'Spare couple change me bredren; spare couple change.' She thinks she is running late for her meeting and rushes up the road as the rain pelts down on a blustery October afternoon.

She is about to hear the stories of learning in this notorious area of cosmopolitan northwest London. As she rushes across the pavement toward a vaguely familiar entrance, she inadvertently drops her open shoulder bag. She is aware of a young oriental man to her left calling out 'DVD! DVD!'. A group of men approaches to her right, swaying and chanting loudly as they drink from beer cans, and at this point she feels a sense of unease. She sees a group of youths wearing hoods directly opposite her at the side of a shop. Further on, at the next corner she sees four young, anxious-looking women sheltering from the rain under the canopy of the corner café, smoking. She holds her coat over her head and simultaneously searches her crowded handbag for an umbrella while charging courageously toward the busy Harltonvale roundabout. She stands in the centre and contemplates the tall blocks of social housing where she spent a considerable time finding her way on her previous visit, and hopes that this time round she will make the right choice and take the exit to the tenants' hall on the ground floor of Blethen House. Clinging on to her A4 folders of carefully prepared consent forms and spare information sheets, she heads in search of the council block that houses the black women's Elders Talk project.

INTERVIEWER: *(shouting out to the women)* Hello there? Where's the entrance to the tenants' hall? *(she hears a muttered response and hurriedly follows the direction of the pointing finger to the ramp)*

SCENE 2: 'The boy set himself off again'

The INTERVIEWER makes her way to the large ramp for wheelchair access to the ground-floor council building and recognizes silver-haired, dark-skinned EDITH, walking out with a large, awkwardly covered plate of steaming hot food in one hand and waving her trademark walking stick up in the air with the other.

EDITH: I coming back, I coming back just now. *(she shouts across to the INTERVIEWER, laughing away in her usual, humorous manner)*

INTERVIEWER: Am I early?

EDITH: Not exactly. The boy set himself off again this morning, police and everyting down here. *(with that, she disappears past the lifts and out of sight)*

Image and text courtesy of Looshan Saltfish

Figure 3: Veronica: 'Learning can raise you high but remember to hold on to your soul'

NARRATOR: I entered the hall to the sound of clanging cutlery and frenzied activity and the aroma of freshly cooked rice and peas being served. I realized I was early for the after-lunch focus group meeting I had so carefully prepared for. I tried to compose myself after my hasty entrance and sat at an empty table at the back of the hall, away from the activity. I noticed how different the hall looked compared to when I first came down here for my meeting with Edith. That cold morning, she had taken me around a large lifeless space occupied by only one woman and a young man in a smart white suit, busily preparing food in the open front kitchen at the far end of the hall. Today, I observed the excitable members of Elders Talk as they lined up to be served their meal by a large lady – Minnie – wearing a bright red, green and gold cap bearing the words 'Trust me!'

The interviewer sits on a chair at the back of the hall. In the background, she can hear the crackling sound system and see the speakers being set up by a colourfully dressed young man. The Bob Marley tune grows gradually louder: 'Saying don't worry, bout a thing, cos every little thing's gonna be alright ...'

The interviewer marvels at the comfortable, heartening scene and feels reassured in a familiar environment. She ponders EDITH's words. What on earth did she mean by: 'The boy set himself off again?' A friendly voice interrupts her thoughts.

CINDY: You want a cup of tea darling?

INTERVIEWER: Oh yes please – one sugar. *(she leans over to find her purse)*

CINDY: Is alright. But £3 for the food ... you can pay more if you like. *(said with a mischievous smile)*

NARRATOR: I looked at the framed photograph of a press cutting with happy smiling faces and read one newspaper caption: 'Our story – our community champion'. I saw an image of a tall, blonde, middle-aged woman wearing a large gold mayoral chain and could make out an Asian man handing over a certificate to a serious-looking black woman dressed in an African robe and an impressive head-dress. I wondered if the receiver of this certificate would be here today to participate in the discussion. Elders Talk holds monthly workshops entitled 'Our Community, Our Stories' for older black women to present their stories. The women are encouraged to hear and discuss each other's stories, told in person or via carefully prepared VHS or audio tape recordings. I sipped the strong tea while waiting for Edith to return and listened to the women talk about the disruption that caused the delay in their weekly activities. I heard one voice say sharply: 'Dem go lock him up tight next time'.

SCENE 3: *A focus on Horatio*

INTERVIEWER: So you have all had a rather trying time this morning, I gather. What happened?

The responses came all at once.

MAUD: Yes. What a time.

ROSA: Me dear child.

EDITH: The boy is so helpful.

ROSA: Always by his mother's side but the young man like playing mas so much.

MAUD: The boy head not right.

SYLVIA: Not right.

MAUD: Not right at all.

This is repeated and stressed by the women.

ROSA: Him well mix up.

DELL: It's the drugs!

EDITH: The boy don't take drugs.

ROSA: Him taking the drugs well.

CINDY: Of course he is. He is taking drugs.

This is also repeated by several women.

EDITH: What evidence you have of that?

JUNE: Yes, what evidence you all have of dat?

CINDY: This is the drugs capital of London. You no hear what the council leader say?

DELL: See it there! Cindy say it all.

NARRATOR: While engaged in their own polyrhythmic realities, it seemed that it would take some time before the women would reach the point where the events of the morning would become clearer, so I decided to guide them back to the agreed discussion.

INTERVIEWER: So thank you for agreeing to talk about your learning in the community In what ways are you learning in the community?

CINDY: *(ignoring the question)* Which part in Dominica your mother come from?

MARLENE: She resemble Beverly, eh?

DELL: *(returning to the previous discussion)* She have it hard with that boy child you know, and she was managing so well on her own.

NARRATOR: Such were the distractions in the research process, my carefully prepared prompts for the group interviews appeared like a parallel, somewhat irrelevant, conversation with myself.

The women continue to ignore the interviewer's questions.

EDITH: She wanted to go to university but instead she sacrifice her life for that boy.

CINDY: From the day the social worker step in, that's when the trouble start.

CYNTHIA: It was just waiting to happen – so much commess.

LILLY: The boy was well bright but the drugs take over.

NARRATOR: I realized the women wanted to take their own time to respond to my question but I persisted in trying to re-focus the discussion.

SCENE 4: *Learning about our history from women in our community*

INTERVIEWER: *(speaking loudly over the women)* And so, how are you learning in the community?

ROSAMOND: *(in a loud, stern voice from the far end of the room)* We are proud of our project.

ROSAMOND is wearing Caribbean dress and a Caribbean head wrap, and has been sitting in the single armchair throughout the interview but has not engaged in the earlier conversations. As she speaks, the other women slowly fall silent. She seems to command a certain level of respect from the women.

INTERVIEWER: Tell me about your project.

The INTERVIEWER is relieved and encouraged by her long-awaited acknowledgement. She looks carefully at the woman and vaguely recognizes her from the photograph on the wall.

ROSAMOND: *(speaking knowledgeably and with a calm, slightly ostentatious tone to her voice)* We talk about our history –'back home', we go way back and we talk of now. We put our history on the map.

INTERVIEWER: How do you do that?

SHIRLEY: Look at this *(thrusts a VHS tape into the hand of the interviewer. She has clearly come prepared for the meeting).*

INTERVIEWER: Is this about the project?

SHIRLEY: It is my story about Crownlands.

INTERVIEWER: Oh, tell me about your story.

SHIRLEY: You have to watch the film.

INTERVIEWER: *(wondering where she would find the appropriate equipment to watch a VHS tape as she would rather connect it to the stories recounted while she is there. She directs another question to all the women)* And so – how are you learning in the project?

SCENE 5: Learning about slavery in our lifetime

NARRATOR: I looked over at the fine-featured woman with pointed nose, dark skin and short black loose curls under a pink woolly hat. I was about to interview her. Other women joined in.

SHIRLEY: I am Shirley and I am a Dougla.

INTERVIEWER: *(pretending to be unfamiliar with an expression she has heard on several occasions from her own mother)* What is a Dougla?

SHIRLEY: Half-black African and half-Indian.

INTERVIEWER: And what is Crownlands? You mentioned it earlier.

SHIRLEY: The sugarcane plantation – 'back home'. It was owned by the King and then the Queen of England. It is on the island of St Lucia. The land is still there but not the regime. It was slavery. My sister lived in the BaHals – the barracks – one long, long building with a separate unit for each family. They did all their cooking, eating and sleeping there and there was a big shop where they bought their provisions and the overseers gave them money for that.

MILDRED: They tell me when you went to visit someone you had to walk right from one end of the BaHal to get to the family unit and then walk all the way down the BaHal to get out again.

CINDY: They just gave the family boxes to sleep on. It was terrible in there. Stink so much I hear. Sometimes there were eight members of one family in one small unit. Like a prison.

INTERVIEWER: Is the building still there?

MILDRED: No – gone long time. Mash down.

SHIRLEY: It was still there in 1978 when I went back for Ma Betty's funeral.

MILDRED: You lie.

SHIRLEY: Yes indeed. The plantation dungeons they use to call it.

INTERVIEWER: So when did it stop?

MILDRED: Well that's for you to find out. You should be telling us young lady!

CINDY: When did slavery stop?

MARLENE: Modern-day slavery.

ROSAMOND: It was not slavery. It gave them a living. It gave them work.

SHIRLEY: Oh, you are so cantankerous sometimes!

ROSAMOND: Vesearse. Move from me! *(other women are laughing)*

NARRATOR: I heard from the women that the British slave masters in St Lucia had built sugarcane barracks on the island – one in Cul de Sac, another in Fonde and another in San Susie. There were many grandfathers working on the plantation. When the black slaves fled and hid in the bushes, attempts to find them proved fruitless. A mandate was eventually introduced to bring in workers ('slaves') from Calcutta in India and the three barracks became dominated by Asian workers. Many intermarried with the local black African Caribbean population and created what is known in parts of the Caribbean as Dougla (half-black African and half-Indian, as explained by Shirley).

On the islands, the people living in the barracks (the BaHals in Bexon) were regarded as poverty-stricken and low class. However, many saved what was left out of the meagre sums paid out to them for food and other basic provisions. Today, their descendants are some of the richest and most respected families on the island and own important local businesses.

The women in Elders Talk had come to the UK from different parts of the Caribbean islands and had clearly been learning from each other's history. I myself had never thought deeply of my grandparents' generation as experiencing slavery. My grandfather was born in 1894 and his father would have been enslaved in the British colonial rule.

SCENE 6: *Learning about the BaHals*

A one-to-one interview with JONETTA (Elders Talk, project worker)

INTERVIEWER: So you have quite a connection with Crownlands?

JONETTA: I was born in the Caribbean in 1958 but came over to the UK as a baby with my mother. My mother's father went on to live in the same housing that his father (a Crownlands plantation worker) was living in and where my maternal grandmother gave birth to my own mother. But mother had sweepingly talked about the BaHals and, for me, it meant a form of housing for the poor. After learning more about it from the other women in the project, I asked an older family relative about it and found out that my mother actually lived there as a very young child. I had stumbled on something which my mother had never ever told me about.

INTERVIEWER: So the project revealed something to you?

JONETTA: I heard about it all the time but I never knew it was so near where my mother lived in Bexon and, yes, I have only found out where it was since the women have been telling their stories. When it was ever mentioned it seemed like it was some place far away – like Souffriere, which is on the other side of the island. My mother was only a child when she lived there but she is constantly cursed by my father's family for coming from the BaHals. They see her as not being worthy of being part of my father's family because of where her family came from. That is so wrong.

INTERVIEWER: Why do you think your mother did not talk about it?

JONETTA: Well it is very clear to me now. My mother is a Dougla and a very proud woman. It must have been awful living in the barracks back then but then she was only a very small child. But I can see the huge stigma attached to having come from the BaHals – it is immense. When my uncles and aunts would say that my mother was a 'poor Bexon girl' – I would always wonder why they would say that because they were also from Bexon, but they did not live in the BaHals. I know now that my family were living there until 1939 but many other families had saved and gotten out and built their modest houses much earlier. She will never tell the other women she lived there.

INTERVIEWER: What fascinating history. Will you be talking to your mother about this new information that you have learnt?

JONETTA: No way, I think it will upset her too much – me bringing it up. My mother is good at giving talks and just last month, she received the community champion award for her work as a volunteer and for 'talking large' to people all over the place. She is quite a legend around here you know. No, I don't want to upset her by talking about the BaHals!

NARRATOR: Jonetta appeared to be protective of her mother Rosamond, and seemed to have been sensitive to her mother's need to disassociate herself from the BaHals, recognizing its obvious association with poverty. The BaHals also presented a sensitive class issue, denoting the stigma of a poorer class or potentially the idea of an 'underclass' in the Bexon community. Rosamond was unlikely to have been proud of that period in her life, and this explained why Jonetta knew nothing of that fact that her mother actually lived in the BaHals as a child. Rosamond was clearly proud of her status as a community champion but did not often engage in the discussion with the other women as if she was placing herself on a higher level. This reserve may have been a way of overcoming her potential sense of earlier inferiority.

SCENE 7: 'Wasted education'

NARRATOR: Turning back to talk to some of the other women, they reverted to the original topic of conversation. I decided to see how this would evolve and what would emerge around ideas of learning.

CYNTHIA: She try and try very hard with the boy. The girls was so good but they gone way with their education and left her with the boy.

JUNE: But not her child?

MARLENE: She try so hard with him but all that education and he don't amount to nothing.

CYNTHIA: You can't say that. The boy is good to his mother. But they should stay and help the mother – they just went away.

EDITH: And the boy was a nice mannersable boy as well.

CYNTHIA: But the boy is ungrateful.

JUNE: It is a crying shame.

INTERVIEWER: Sounds so very sad.

EDITH: When you see him like that, you must say nothing. You have to put up with the noise. Just leave him alone. You can say hello but don't disrespect him. Ignore him and pretend you don't see him. Minnie is a very disciplined. She is an organized and reliable woman but when she get mad, she provoke him about his education. You can't rebuke that boy. She can't stop humiliating the boy. He was doing well to get in university and had a good opportunity and she wanted so much to go to university herself. He just wasted his education.

CINDY: They deport him twice. Once from Jamaica and the other time from New York.

INTERVIEWER: From Jamaica?

CINDY: She send him to his grandmother – it never work.

EDITH: She send him to the aunty in New York – he carry on bad there too.

INTERVIEWER: Deported from New York?

EDITH: Yes – to England. He was born right here. Yes, Middlesex hospital – just down the road.

CINDY: The same hospital dat destroy his life.

EDITH: All that education.

DELL: He is always by her side.

ROSAMOND: He is her life – right here at the centre.

NARRATOR: It was then that I realized that Horatio was the smartly dressed young man in the white suit I had seen in the kitchen on my first visit, helping his mother, Minnie, prepare lunch for the members of Elders Talk. He might have also been the young man I had earlier observed setting up the speaker box. But what of Edith's reference to: 'Set himself off'?

Toward the end of the interview with CINDY, the INTERVIEWER asks about the incident that morning.

INTERVIEWER: Why were the police here this morning?

CINDY: Minnie let rip into Horatio again.

INTERVIEWER: What do you mean?

CINDY: She was cursing him and calling him 'rubbish' and saying how he wasted his education and he just set himself off and this was not the first time.

INTERVIEWER: His mother?

CINDY: His mother is in charge of organizing the meals at the luncheon clubs. He gets epileptic fits when he is severely upset. He had a 'runnings' with his mother this morning. The last time it happened, we were preparing for the second year of the Harlstonvale carnival when Horatio was about to give his talk. He set himself off back then too. Screaming, cursing and shouting at everybody.

Image and text courtesy of Cynthia Charlemagne

Figure 8: Cynthia – 'A focus on my son's education and a happy life for me now'

NARRATOR: The area of North West London where the women volunteer is notorious for youth gangs, robbery and 'black-on-black' crime. When the police received a call concerning a young black man 'causing trouble', apparently they came to the scene in large numbers. 'He set him off again' means he caused himself to become distressed and agitated. It also implied that he was to blame for becoming agitated – not his mother, not the police, not anyone but himself. However, the explanations given, as I heard them, were that 'she' (Minnie) had probably set him off again. She may have taken her frustration out on him and, although he was loyal and supportive to his mother, Horatio was aware of her disappointment over the outcome of his education. Other comments suggested that he might be suffering from depression as a result of failures and disappointments in his own life and his inability to make Minnie proud of him. But despite inferences, the Elders Talk members provided sisterly support to Minnie. In the women's eyes, Minnie was considered right to talk to her son in whatever way she chose, not reflecting that perhaps she should allow for Horatio's particular problem, such as epilepsy or depression. In the women's eyes, he was 'born here' and therefore expected to do better. 'They ran away with their education and left her with the boy.' Horatio's siblings seemed to have done well but had also come under criticism for leaving too much responsibility with their mother. It was evident that Minnie had placed significant importance on educating her children at the expense of her own education. 'She wanted to go to university but she sacrificed her life for that boy.' Minnie's story (as told by others) highlighted the conflict between different aspirations and roles: motherhood and access to education.

Review of Act 2

This act has introduced the cosmopolitan local environment in which the community centre is located and where the interviews were to take place. Scene 2 described the cultural features of the project and centre and its community learning setting, and exposed the nature of the researcher's initial encounter with her research participants. Scene 3 described the participants' insistence on focusing on a mother's sacrifice and commitment to educating her son, who now struggled with day-to-day living in the community. In Scene 4 the participants discussed their informal learning activities within the Elders Talk project and how they are able to explore and share their history. Scene 5 presented the women's learning about modern-day slavery on a sugarcane plantation 'back home' on one West Indian Island. Scene 6 provided further insights into events occurring back home as they recounted stories of poverty and social disadvantage. In Scene 7 the women discussed a boy's 'wasted education' and returned to a mother's disappointment in light of the high expectations she had of her son doing well, at the expense of her own education.

Smith (2000) encapsulates the rationale for the growing body of work in black feminist epistemology. Collins (1990) similarly points to the diverse, previously hidden, contributions that black women are able to make to an important area of theoretical development, and argues that, in developing black feminist thought: 'Understanding the complexity of black women's activism requires understanding, not only of the need to address more than one form of oppression, but the significance of how singular and multiple forms of oppression are organised' (Collins, 2000a: 218).

For older black women, opportunities to participate equitably in learning are likely to be affected by multiple factors such as racism, caring responsibilities, sexism and ageism, all of which have negative consequences for educational achievements and later aspirations. In the UK, this intersectionality of race, class and gender is identified by Carby (1997) and also Christian (1988) as significantly affecting the role and social position of black women in community settings. Collins (1990) theorizes multiple layers of black feminist interpretation, which incorporates black feminism, womanism, Afrocentric feminism and Africana womanism. Together these construct a different reality and a distinct way of gathering information about the lives of groups of black women. This moves the debate away from the intersectional categories identified by British scholars that potentially encourage deficit models through their negative connotations. The different reality proposed by Collins also opens up the experience of shared cultural identity, emphasizing various intersections of multiple, polyrhythmic realities (Sheared, 1996; Alfred, 2002) able to shape the lives of both the researcher and the researched.

Polyrhythmic realities across black feminist epistemology promote and give voice to an ethic of shared accountability and social responsibility for black women, which Africana womanist theorist Hudson-Weems (2004) states is fundamental in meeting needs in the wider black community. At the heart of Africana womanist theory is the recognition that black feminism should attempt to acknowledge the involvement of black men in a collective struggle to tackle oppression. Hudson-Weems points out that we should refrain from taking our starting point from other feminist commentators and, as black women, should continually seek to develop our own unique voice in the struggle for gender equality. According to Hudson-Weems, black feminism should be focused on the experiences, struggles, needs and desires of Africana women of the African diaspora; these must be at the forefront of our struggles before we consider gender, community or class issues. She stresses that 'Africana Womanism commands an African-centred perspective of African women's lives – their historical, current and future interaction with their community' (Hudson-Weems, 1998: 82).

On the other hand, Collins (2000b) highlights the interwoven influence of sexism and racism and advocates that black feminist thought be critical social theory, reflecting power relationships and empowerment. She insists that it is an analysis of a response to injustice that remains at the core of its principles. She concludes that black feminist thought seeks to embrace and address the common oppressions of sexism, racism, sexuality and class, and affirms: 'Maintaining the invisibility of Black women and our ideas not only in the United States, but in Africa, the Caribbean, South America, Europe, and other places where Black women now live, has been critical in maintaining social inequalities' (Collins, 2000a: 5).

But how might black feminist thought relate to the reality of the lives of black British Caribbean women who arrived in Britain in the 1950s, many of whom came in their early twenties, experiencing exploitation of their labour (Carby, 1997) to build up the economy (Lewis, 2001)? Similarly, I reflected on how black feminist thought related to those older black women who had had 'a good education back home' but who ended up in the UK working as cleaners and auxiliary nurses in the National Health Service. The framing and interconnected (Brah and Phoenix, 2004) nature of their racialized and gendered experiences are hard to separate from their wider socio-economic exclusion (Baksh-Soodeen, 1994; Reddock, 2007). The later chapters of this study will draw on both Collins's and Hudson-Weems's ideas to help interpret experiences of education and womanist activism among such women. Nevertheless, from the discussion above, I would argue that it is important to understand black feminism combined with underlying experiences of oppression and the ability to share and express knowledge of such oppression. These stories show how, through sharing and knowledge, activism may enable change to take place among a community of black women. The next act in this chapter continues to highlight the significance of black feminist thought.

Black women, feminist thought and difference

Black women's desire to voice their experiences and collectively organise themselves is articulated through the key sites of motherhood and family, education, employment and community activism.

(Reynolds, 2005: 19)

Collins (2000a) acknowledges that developing black feminist thought involves searching for its expression in alternative institutional locations and among women who are not commonly perceived as intellectuals. This highlights a valuable perspective offered in this book.

In their study of black Caribbean mothers and their children, both Reynolds (2005) and Abrams (2010) point to the importance placed on education by Caribbean mothers. For the Caribbean mother, the role of the teacher is sacrosanct (Mirza, 2009; Johnson-Bailey and Alfred, 2006) and education is considered vital not only for her own personal development but also for the survival of her children in contemporary urban society. Such unquestionable support for the teacher is endorsed by Alfred (2003), who found in her study of British Caribbean immigrant women that culture and early socialization during schooling in the country of origin greatly influenced the later learning experiences of the black woman in the host country. In such circumstances, dedication to learning and education was perceived as of primary importance. However, in the UK, the struggle to escape poverty (Platt, 2007) has continued to haunt certain ethnic groups from generation to generation, making dedication to formal learning beyond basic schooling highly problematic in the lives of black women in particular (Goulbourne and Chamberlain, 2001; Reynolds, 2005). This raises the question: what role might exist for the older black woman in helping others escape poverty while at the same time developing her learning? Exploring the political and social activism of older black women may shed light on this question but first we need to consider the theoretical framework for understanding black women's activism. Black women 'have known that their lives in some ways incorporated goals that white middle-class women were striving for, but race and class privilege, of course, reshaped the meaning of those goals profoundly' (Smith, 2000: 21).

ACT 3: Speaking to represent: A story of writing in the community

CAST OF CHARACTERS

NARRATOR	The INTERVIEWER speaks to the audience, as an aside
INTERVIEWER	Speaks directly to the characters
DELORIS	Aged 59, from Jamaica
MADGE	Aged 57, from Barbados
TRUDY	Aged 55, from St Vincent
GLORIA	Aged 77, from Jamaica
FLORA	Aged 78, from Jamaica

SCENE 1: *Arrival*

The INTERVIEWER drives down a leafy suburban road in Sunnyvale, Middlehampton, on a crisp bright Saturday morning to conduct her planned one-to-one interview at the home of the chairperson of the local African Caribbean Women's Centre. She pulls up at a large semi-detached house with white pillars and cannot fail to see the bright red, shiny sports car parked in the driveway. As she sits behind the wheel of her shabby little black Polo, she wonders whether or not to park alongside the red sports car, but finds a discreet parking space lower down the road. While walking back up the road to the house, she observes an assortment of similar looking large houses with cars in the driveways, and that places for visitors to park were sparse. On pressing the whimsical doorbell, she notices the small marble plaque by the front door bearing the words: 'Sunnyvale Villa'. A few seconds later, DELORIS comes to greet her at the front door and is now vigorously shaking her hand.

SCENE 2: *Welcome*

DELORIS: *(Deloris is a tall, slim, light-skinned, older black woman, wearing a long cream-coloured dress)* Welcome, do come in. *(speaking in a regal, assertive tone of voice)* We are all in the kitchen, waiting for you.

NARRATOR: I was a little taken aback by the 'we', as I was under the impression that I was about to conduct a one-to-one interview with Deloris Hunt – but I said nothing. On entering the spacious hallway, I noticed the glamorous studio photographs of Deloris lining the walls and was about to compliment her when she swiftly ushered me through the luxurious lounge with its minimalist furnishings, adorned with a large framed photograph of a young man in graduation robe and cap, holding his degree certificate.

DELORIS: *(beckoning INTERVIEWER down to the open-plan kitchen)* Come through, come through. *(speaking with an educated upper-class English accent)* My mother could not resist being part of this, and Madge has something to say as well.

NARRATOR: Well, I thought to myself – something to say – about what precisely? And who was Madge?

DELORIS: *(regally spoken as if to a large sophisticated audience)* I want you to meet everyone and yes they are all from the Caribbean as well and can share their thoughts with you and, no – they don't mind you recording the interview. As volunteers at the Women's Centre, they are quite used to that kind of thing anyway. *(laughs)* You and I can then have a one-to-one later on.

The INTERVIEWER thinks quickly, looks over at the four smartly dressed older women sitting around the solid oak table laden with magazines, books and a neat green folder in front of each of them.

INTERVIEWER: *(trying not to look surprised)* Oh. That sounds wonderful.

DELORIS: This is Trudy. I am writing the article about her for the women's magazine.

TRUDY: *(laughing)* I now must find a photograph.

DELORIS: *(in a playful but serious tone)* Find a photograph! Absolutely not! You must have a new one taken.

DELORIS: This is my mother Gloria, as you probably gathered. And this is my aunt Flora and here is my neighbour, Madge, from down the road.

GLORIA (DELORIS's mother) passes the INTERVIEWER a green folder.

NARRATOR: The women to be interviewed (unexpectedly) might be perceived as black middle-class. Three have children educated at university, own their own homes and are now volunteering for pleasure in the community. Deloris, Madge and Trudy arrived in the UK with their mothers as a toddler and all experienced the British education system.

As I opened the folder and looked at the carefully arranged information about the project and facts about the women, I felt slightly uncomfortable with Deloris's painstaking organization but I was glad to be meeting older black Caribbean women, and hoped I had brought along more than one consent form.

DELORIS: These women provide me with the inspiration I need when writing for the magazine.

INTERVIEWER: So. Are you all happy to participate in the research and has Deloris filled you in on all the background?

NARRATOR: It seemed to me that I would not need to probe too much with my topics and was beginning to feel comfortable about conducting an organized interview where all my research questions would be attended to.

SCENE 3: *Group interview*

INTERVIEWER: What does lifelong learning mean to you?

MADGE: It is everything we do.

DELORIS: The sorts of things the Women's Resource Centre puts on are all examples: health and healthy eating and lifestyle workshops; a lot of information on diabetes – because that is a real killer in our community. Everything we do, generally, learning about how to stay healthy, by providing good examples from inside the community. At the centre the women have access to computers, photocopying and printing but as you can see I have a computer, photocopier and printer in the lounge.

GLORIA: We do have quite a lot of equipment at the centre – scanners, computers, a fax machine but the building is so untidy, dirty and noisy.

MADGE: All sorts of women drop in there from all over and we cannot always learn because of the noise.

FLORA: And at times it is very crowded.

GLORIA: You expect that at that kind of centre.

DELORIS: I agree. It is so much more convenient to get together here.

TRUDY: We all drive so it is not a problem coming here to Deloris's place.

FLORA: And here you can get a nice cup of tea from a china cup!

GLORIA: And not a chipped mug.

All the women laugh.

DELORIS: It really is not my kind of environment.

The INTERVIEWER re-focuses on lifelong learning.

INTERVIEWER: So about lifelong learning. What do you do? How are you learning?

NARRATOR: Social class and status seemed to be factors in choosing to gather at Deloris's home – particularly in the way certain sentiments were expressed by the women, such as, 'all sorts of women drop in' and 'that kind of centre' and 'not my kind of environment'. The women had found a range of 'legitimate' reasons for gathering at Deloris's home but the underlying reason appeared to be class. This effectively created an exclusive, self-selected learning group.

SCENE 4: 'A touch of class'

DELORIS: I write the Caribbean section for the Women's Resource Centre magazine. I am on the editorial board and have to take responsibility for writing the story but the women tell me as much as possible. The centre allows me two pages of text and the other page allocated usually contains short reports, advertisements, events, diary dates and so on. I let Liza – the Australian centre co-ordinator – check it all for accuracy for me because it is always good to do that. Here is my draft of Trudy's story. *(gives the interviewer an A4 typed sheet to read)*

INTERVIEWER: Is this the article about coping with diabetes?

TRUDY: Yes but it's not about me, it's about my father, who has Type 2 diabetes. I spoke to Deloris about how I managed and what I have to do to look after him. My father is 80 and he also has glaucoma.

DELORIS: It is her story but other women will clearly benefit from reading the article.

INTERVIEWER: So you are writing factual material?

DELORIS: I usually do but I did a piece once about healthy Caribbean cooking and somehow I made a negative comment about the dasheen and you know the women had a right go at me for disrespecting a part of our staple diet! I wrote that there were some concerns about the dasheen, that eating a large amount was dangerous because it contained some form of harmful colouring.

GLORIA: Colouring! How can something natural contain colouring?

FLORA: And how can anyone eat too much of it? Dasheen was growing in such abundant quantities back home.

DELORIS: But if there was nothing else to eat!

TRUDY: All our lives we have been eating dasheen.

GLORIA: Yes, we were raised since time and memorial *(she has changed the expression 'time immemorial' to 'time and memorial')*, eating yams and dasheens and green banana and now you are telling us that our food is poisonous!

DELORIS: No, rather that there may be some foods eaten in large quantities that may be dangerous to our health.

GLORIA: Some might see it as offensive that you should write this.

TRUDY: (*spoken in a highfalutin exaggerated tone*) Green bananas contain a great deal of nutrients and we all need iron.

NARRATOR: The women's speech appeared to me to be deliberately exaggerated as if they were projecting perfect British accents with a touch of class (Maguire, 1999) in their role as educators.

SCENE 5: *One-to-one interview with Deloris*

INTERVIEWER: So Deloris, tell me about your readership.

DELORIS: We have a list of around 160 women – not just black women. There are 180 names but not all of them come to the meetings of course. When we have the big events, like a drama, you will be surprised to see how many turn up. We had a sickle cell evening not too long ago and we invited some special guests from London – the TV host and an ex-boxer came to speak – he proved quite popular actually. But it's all lifelong learning.

INTERVIEWER: May I ask you again, what does lifelong learning mean to you?

DELORIS: It means the right thing to be doing. I mean why should we stop?

INTERVIEWER: And are you enjoying learning outside of an institution?

DELORIS: (*seeming to instinctively understand the INTERVIEWERS's question*) Immensely!

INTERVIEWER: So what exactly is the nature of this learning that takes place while you are volunteering at the centre?

DELORIS: In writing for the magazine I have to get it right. Not just listening to the women but checking facts is quite a deep process of learning. When we were having the debates about the dasheen, I did not know that there was so much information available – studies and workshops all over the world. I was constantly finding new information.

INTERVIEWER: Using the Internet?

DELORIS: Young people today do not know how lucky they are. They hardly have to look far for information. All they have to do is just click on a button. Is it any wonder they get bored and get up to all sorts!

INTERVIEWER: To what extent is your learning impacting on the wider community?

DELORIS: It is a two-way process: I write an opinion and I get feedback from the others. Some women were not happy with the articles I did on the earthquake relief efforts in Haiti. They felt I spent too much time on it and less time on the hurricane relief efforts following the most recent hurricane in Jamaica.

INTERVIEWER: Were they right?

DELORIS: They might have been but I knew less about that and I only put my information together based on facts around me. My view was the women were not all that interested in the Haiti situation, not as much as the Jamaican situation – but it is all learning.

NARRATOR: The women in the room spoke about their activities at the Women's Resource Centre and were generally very courteous and respectful of each other, even when they disagreed, allowing one another time to provide a contribution to a discussion. Polyrhythmic realities were not clearly evident among the social interactions of this group of women. They did not interrupt each other's contributions. They waited their turn and allowed one another to speak. However, when the subject of formal education and the lack of qualifications of a senior Caribbean politician were raised, it did not take long before polyrhythmic realities came into play among these sophisticated women.

SCENE 6: Public life and respect for education

As the group interview comes to a close, a West Indian newspaper story becomes the subject of discussion.

GLORIA: De man dou av no qualifications and shouda never be representing de people dem!

ALL: *(speaking all at once)* No qualifications wat so ever!

DELORIS: De man is a jinal!

TRUDY: *(shouting in a high pitched voice)* Bobolos too!

Everyone laughs.

GLORIA: Me hear say him dou even hav school sets!

More hysterical laughter from all.

ALL: No qualifications.

ALL: *(repeating)* No qualifications.

FLORIA: You tink dis ah cud appen ina JA!

INTERVIEWER: Excuse me, can you repeat that?

FLORA: No star. Him wud a av run fe im life! *(she points her right hand with two closed fingers up in the air twice and shouts)* Bom, Bom!

The INTERVIEWER is ignored.

DELORIS: Never apen ina JA.

TRUDY: Tell dem sis.

NARRATOR: I was taken aback by the women's sudden switch from the perfectly constructed English accent to the rather raw Caribbean patois. It was as if the women had found a whole new language and had just revealed it. Although I understood the dialect, I found it hard to keep up with their unfamiliar pronunciation. I felt completely shut out, and it was clear that the women were intentionally excluding me. Curiously, I had never felt excluded to that degree by the language of the women featured in the earlier acts. Here I was in the audience, set apart.

INTERVIEWER: Which country is this?

TRUDY: Pure scandalous, pure carry on.

The INTERVIEWERS's question is ignored.

MADGE: The man saying to everybody: you don't need education!

FLORA: Wat a terrible ting.

DELORIS: Im even favor Duppy! *(pushes her shoulders back, and clenches her fists in a 'manly fashion' in her elegant cream-coloured silk dress)* De man is a mockery! We caa stan fi dat! *(everyone laughs again)*

There is a moment of silence as the INTERVIEWER gazes at the women and closes her notebook.

DELORIS: *(reassuming her regal British accent)* But I cannot understand how and why he was put in charge in the first place.

TRUDY: It is such an embarrassing situation that I don't believe it to be true.

GLORIA: In politics so much can be invented.

TRUDY: That is so very true!

The INTERVIEWER appears baffled but somewhat relieved at the return to 'normality'.

MADGE: He must have been qualified – surely he would not have been allowed to hold such a position?

FLORA: This is politics.

DELORIS: If he was a woman he would never have gotten a foot in the door!

GLORIA: Eugenia Charles I am sure has all sorts of qualifications.

MADGE: But he is in a senior position!

FLORA: Anything can happen in politics.

DELORIS: You mean polytricks.

Everyone laughs.

GLORIA: But the islanders must feel terrible to know that he is in the role but with no formal academic qualifications!

INTERVIEWER: Is that a fact?

TRUDY: No it is only gossip

DELORIS: Can you imagine if the UK appointed a man to a similar position with no formal qualifications?

TRUDY: But he is good at his job.

GLORIA: That is not the issue.

The INTERVIEWER remains silent as the women continue uninterrupted.

FLORA: You know it is wrong and the people have made a terrible mistake which I hope they will not repeat.

GLORIA: It is so wrong.

MADGE: You have so many more persons with the world of qualification and they are useless at their jobs – what is worse than that? He is good at his job!

DELORIS: But why are you sticking up for him?!

Everyone laughs.

NARRATOR: The women were all born in the Caribbean and they all had such perfect English accents. But, clearly at any time, they could switch to

Caribbean patois. I reflected on the switch and felt it to be a reflection of the collective strength of the women, sticking with each other in a shared belief that they were unwilling to have challenged. They held a view and they wanted time to indulge in social interaction with each other to show their disapproval and express their views on meritocracy. I surmised that if they felt that I, as an outsider (the knowledgeable researcher), might challenge their contempt of the man under discussion, they might not have a chance to express the condemnation they felt was warranted. This was also a feature of polyrhythmic reality: the sisterly support and trivializing ways in which they addressed serious matters. Reverting to Caribbean patois was, I felt, one sure way of shutting out the interviewer. Although I acknowledge that the women may have been aware that I could speak patois, they also knew that in my professional role as researcher I would be unlikely to use patois to communicate with them. Thus they could keep me outside this discussion until they secured their ground.

Review of Act 3

This act was a marked contrast to the earlier stories, where the majority of the women spoke in their own Caribbean dialects about particular situations. In this act, the Caribbean roots of the participants were not always clear in their middle-class speech until, through passion and excitement, they reverted to displaying their polyrhythmic realities and used the patois of 'back home'.

Image and text courtesy of Looshan Saltfish

Figure 5: Eugenia – 'Oh how I yearn for womanist teachings from my older sisters'

Lifelong learning as informal learning

The women in Act 3 were learning in informal ways. Field refers to this as the type of lifelong learning that is self-directed and undertaken by individuals in the course of their daily lives (Field, 2006a: 5). Similarly, Morgan-Klein and Osborne (2007: 14) describe informal learning as 'learning that either takes place outside of institutions' or is defined by some other element of 'informality', such as non-certified learning, contrasting it with the trend to certificate informal or community-based learning.

Participating in informal learning has been linked to increased levels of practical community association, such as involvement with tenants' boards, engagement as school governors and wider grassroots action, positively encouraging citizenship (Crick, 2000b; Jackson, 2007; Annette and Mayo, 2009). Such activities can lead to greater political awareness and growing critical consciousness (Freire, 1999). Informal learning forms an important and integral part of lifelong learning (Cropley, 1980) and, in the context of older learners in the third (50–75) and fourth (over 75) ages, can best be described as the type of learning that takes place in social networks, through 'membership of voluntary networks and organisations of various kinds, where individuals and groups pursue the things that interest them' (Field, 2006a: 166).

However, opportunities for such social networks to thrive are fast diminishing for older people as a result of government cuts to adult and community learning and the voluntary sector more generally (Milbourne, 2013). Such a situation impacts on older black communities to a greater degree as they are often excluded from the wide range of informal learning activities available to other groups.

Social capital, social exclusion and the benefits of lifelong learning

Education and community participation strategies have been regarded as significant approaches to tackling social exclusion (Sen, 2000), reinforcing the significance of links between learning and community participation. As Clayton explains:

> *There are many forms that such partnerships can and do take: involvement with community organisations, tenants' associations, women's centres and so on. These can help to reach people with little contact with officialdom. In addition, part of the value of using local people, including those who themselves are members*

of socially excluded groups, is that this enables their voice to be heard: they can make their own expert input.

(Clayton, 2006: 6)

There are over 15,000 black and ethnic minority organizations in Britain (Jones, 2010), many of them locally based. These organizations offer access to resources and social capital, which is increasingly significant in the lives of older people at risk of isolation. However, Campbell and McLean show that the 'construction of ethnic identities – within a context of institutionalised racism – both the material and symbolic levels – makes it unlikely that people will view local community organisations or networks as representative of their interests and needs' (Campbell and McLean, 2002: 3).

Belonging and social networks, like community (Brent, 2009), are therefore both inclusive and exclusive, and require levels of trust, shared interests and networks to enable inclusive and potentially emancipatory activities to develop. According to Putnam (2000), when trust and social networks flourish, individuals, neighbourhoods and even nations prosper. But this view is challenged by research that examines micro-level engagement, such as Jackson's (2007) and also Brent's work (2009), highlighting competing community interests that create insiders and outsiders in community organizations. Schuller *et al.* (2004) also describe how people who engage in learning are more likely to be active citizens.

Mayo (2000) highlights the increasing interest in developing connections between lifelong learning and community capacity-building, whereby so-called deficits in bridging social capital can be 'remedied'. She argues that 'policies for the development of social capital have been linked with strategies to combat social exclusion and facilitate wider processes of democratic renewal' (Mayo, 2000: 24). However, as Garmanikow and Green (1999) also stress, such policies often discount the value of bonding social capital among different social and cultural groups and invariably assume deficits in social capital or resources among poorer or less advantaged neighbourhoods. In this way they avoid the structural or institutional analyses for assumed lack of cultural resources, which can be remedied by individual and community agency (Milbourne, 2002).

For Britain's diverse communities, recent strategies intended to tackle community cohesion may offer benefits in developing resources to strengthen the mechanisms that promote bridging social capital (Field, 2005). But they may also disregard existing bonds and networks, which may be less visible to outsiders. The idea of building social capital in diverse neighbourhoods frequently implies a deficit model of alternative approaches and cultures that may exist there (Milbourne, 2009), whereas the social networks and experiences emerging from community learning at local levels may be rich but sit more comfortably outside a middle-class habitus. This leads me to question the apparently inclusive rhetoric in lifelong learning policies and whether they have failed to address the needs of the excluded groups.

Dilemmas in the research process

In conducting my research I was acutely aware of my social and moral responsibilities and my aims for integrity in all phases of the research process. My research questions revolved around my relationships with my research participants. Did the women have confidence in me? Did they trust me? What values was I bringing to the research? Was I making implicit judgements about participants? As Milbourne (2013: 66) highlights, formal codes may guide conduct but 'a willingness to recognise moral obligation underpinned by the demands of social linkage' may be more helpful for building trust in research relationships in community-based settings and thereby enhance information-sharing.

One example in particular illustrates the kind of issues and dilemmas (Sultana, 2007) that arose. As I was beginning a one-to-one interview at a Caribbean cultural community centre, one participant asked if I would interview an older black Caribbean male because, she advised me, he resented the idea that the research was targeted at women only and felt this was hugely discriminatory. She relayed to me his feelings of wanting to be involved and felt that he had a right to be part of the process. It appeared he had given the woman an ultimatum and, as a result, she was pleading with me to accommodate his wishes. Although I felt that this placed me in a rather awkward position, I was mindful of safeguarding my research relationship with my female research participant, knowing that she needed an answer from me before proceeding with her interview. She was clearly fearful of how she might be treated by her male colleague if he was not allowed into the process. She felt that my offer of speaking with him separately concerning the nature of the research would be insufficient, as he wanted to participate in a full interview with me. I realized that my actions would matter greatly and I wondered about the appropriateness of going ahead with the man's interview just to keep the peace. I finally agreed to a short interview with him – perhaps inappropriate for the nature of my study but it taught me a lesson for the future about how I prepare the ground prior to conducting this kind of research.

Such issues of power and ethical concerns continued to pose dilemmas throughout the research process (Lieblich, 1996) but I improved my ability to handle such situations as the study progressed. I reflected on this event in my research notebook and how I would handle a future situation if it were to occur again. The interviews held with women in their homes were relaxed and more reflective. At community centres they were tenser and this was often the result of men wanting to participate. Other ethical dilemmas for me concerned the extent to which the women participants were fully aware of the reasons for the research and its potential benefits. Feedback from earlier research into health and social care among a black elderly population (Butt and O'Neil, 2004; Sin, 2004) reported participants complaining about being 'researched to death'. To what extent was I replicating this experience? To encourage willingness, trust and confidence in the research process, I had previously shared with the women the fact that there was limited research available into lifelong learning and black women of their generation. I re-stated that older black women learners were likely to be playing significant roles in their communities but research had yet to acknowledge this. Their input was therefore invaluable. I stressed to them that as the research was focused on *them*, I believed it was important to hear their views and experiences in the absence of their male counterparts. Such a way forward was likely to encourage confidence for many of the women participants. I finally expressed to the women that the roles they were playing in the community were important ones and, as such, required acknowledging. It was important for me to restate these issues. Following such explanations I was able to make progress with the interviews.

Chapter 4

The heart of the race

ACT 4: Taking on board the establishment: A story of learning for challenge

CAST OF CHARACTERS

NARRATOR	The INTERVIEWER speaks to the audience, as an aside
INTERVIEWER	Speaks directly to the characters
YVONNE	Aged 61, from St Kitts
IONA	Aged 72, from Jamaica
DOROTHY	Aged 73, from Jamaica
LETICIA	Aged 60, from Guyana
JUNE	Aged 52, from Trinidad
MARY	Aged 70, St Kitts
AMOS	Receptionist at the Regeneration Centre

SCENE 1: *The slow regeneration of Lossington*

The INTERVIEWER is standing in the middle of a large open field on the Lossington estate in Northwest England, about to prepare for a group interview with the Black Elders' group. She moves forward toward an empty wooden bench and as she goes to sit down she notices the emblem on the bench, which reads: 'Lossington Challenge: Working for the Community'. She looks at the new-build, low rise, light-blue painted flats before her and contrasts them with the tall towering greyness of the old blocks surrounding the scene. She observes the quaint architecture of the desolate city garden at the centre of her view, a design obviously worked on enthusiastically once but now abandoned and uninspiring. The shops in the distance look old and drab and she wonders how long before the shiny new flats too will look the same on this expansive priority housing estate.

SCENE 2: *Assertiveness at the community centre*

NARRATOR: I rang the buzzer of the Regeneration Centre for a few minutes without getting an answer, then slowly pushed the slightly open door to see a bright hall with a sense of newness about it. There was a fresh smell of paint. A pool table stood close to the wall and two stacks of chairs covered in plastic wrapping were located against the wall. I walked cautiously toward the empty reception desk when I heard a loud booming voice coming from behind me.

AMOS: The centre is closed!

INTERVIEWER: *(a little startled)* I have come for a meeting with the black women's group.

AMOS: The centre is closed! Lady, I tell you there is no meeting here today.

INTERVIEWER: But I have …

AMOS: *(interrupting)* Listen, they are not here today, Wednesdays only.

INTERVIEWER: I have a group meeting with them at 10, but I am slightly early.

AMOS: *(in a sharp tone)* Well there's nothing in the book my lady!

NARRATOR: As I reached for my phone in my coat pocket, I heard the cheery voices of Caribbean women giggling as they entered the hall. One voice calls out: 'There she is. Come to interview us.' I then received a cheery greeting from the women, who ushered me toward a door bearing the sign 'Small training room'. Then I heard the booming male voice again.

AMOS: *(admonishing and waving a notebook in the air)* Listen, you all have to sign in.

NARRATOR: The interchange began, already offering me insights into how different roles were asserted at this centre.

MARY: But let us open up the door first, Amos. You so facety.

AMOS: No come right now. Too much slackness going on round here these days.

DOROTHY: We coming just now. Relax nah man.

YVONNE: I see you have not yet unpacked these chairs, Amos. This must be done in time for the meeting.

DOROTHY: I hope you have put that boiler on already.

AMOS: Come on. Come on. Sign in please. Every time is de same ting, all you carry on like you all run de damn place.

NARRATOR: This first exchange put in my mind an impulse to begin my questions by asking about roles.

INTERVIEWER: Please tell me about the roles you carry out in the community.

MARY: I am the treasurer of the women's group and a New Vision Board member.

IONA: I come for de course and I mekde teas and sandwiches for the meetings.

YVONNE: I am a board member and I am doing the course.

DOROTHY: I am the chairperson of the women's group and also a board member.

LETICIA: I am the vice-chair of the women's group.

JUNE: I co-ordinate the training for the women in the block – the old housing blocks that is.

SCENE 3: Learning the language of the board

INTERVIEWER: Do you do all this on a voluntary basis?

MARY: It is all voluntary. We call on the elderly during the week but we are really a pressure group because the women in the blocks are isolated and on their own. When we got the grant from the board it all went for the ten-weeks' course.

DOROTHY: But we did get the money for any expenses associated with the course – like lunches and teas and coffee ...

LETICIA: And face make-up if you get your way.

Everyone laughs.

DOROTHY: Well you know I like to look good.

INTERVIEWER: Tell me about the course.

MARY: The courses are to help with our communication skills and they are run by Training for Empowerment. We come to the centre for two hours every week for the programme. We don't get to have our group meetings when we are on the course but we see each other more often.

JUNE: We're not sure if it will run next year as the money comes from the Challenge under-spend money but the board want to see more black women taking part and getting a certificate.

IONA: We ave two more weeks to go.

YVONNE: Our trainer is Tatiana and she's very helpful and very experienced.

LETICIA: Yes she is a very bright girl.

MARY: There are words which we don't understand and our teacher is good at explaining things to us and training us.

DOROTHY: How can they expect us to agree to anything if we don't even understand what some of these words mean?

MARY: Like procarement.

JUNE: Procurement.

YVONNE: And 'virement'.

LETICIA: And 'capital funding'.

DOROTHY: Oh we all know that one.

JUNE: But you all only just get to understand 'underspend!'

Everyone laughs.

SCENE 4: A focus for learning

INTERVIEWER: So you are really learning on the course?

IONA: We ave a lot of fun and we learn so much from Tatiana and from each other and I ave more confidence since I ave been on the course. She put us on camera and we watch ourselves giving performances *(laughing)*. We ad just a few of us to start with but now der are many younger women wanting it but der is no room.

MARY: Tatiana is very strict with us. We read the papers aloud and each one read a section so that we understand it. I don't know how we will get on when she goes because we won't do it when she is gone.

YVONNE: But why not? We should be able to.

DOROTHY: It is hard for us. We need her to guide us.

JUNE: You know we cannot get her back. The money was only a one-off.

DOROTHY: Babygirl, I think we had better learn how to motivate each other. Our problem is we are all too judgemental of each other.

All the women laugh.

NARRATOR: I observed how most of the women felt that learning away from the teacher was not easy and questioned their own ability to sustain motivation.

DOROTHY: The teacher always asks us to bring the papers from the meetings and we have to account for things and tell her what took place and how we asked our questions and how we felt. But at the end of the day it is up to us; she can only guide us.

YVONNE: She is really worth the money.

MARY: She will get paid the second instalment when she finish the work. Her mother is from Manchester you know. Her father is a black Jamaican but I hear they separate long time. She is a young woman with a good head on her shoulders.

IONA: She conscious. I like to see young people dat know where dey come from and where dey going.

LETITIA: She is roots and culture.

INTERVIEWER: So about the course ...

IONA: The course really opened us up to many tings. We even feel OK to ask dem to put things in bigger print for some of us *(laughing and looking at Dorothy)*.

DOROTHY: Now when I get my reports I look forward to reading it.

IONA: If we see someting we are not appy with – we tell dem in advance so it can go on de agenda.

MARY: Before they refused to allow us to speak or raise our points. When we were unhappy with the Challenge Walkers and the way they were behaving and roughing up the young kids – like they were police officers.

NARRATOR: When the women refer to 'them' and 'they', I deduced they are referring to other members of the Challenge Board.

DOROTHY: But some of us did get very angry.

YVONNE: You, you mean!

DOROTHY: But sister, they did not want to listen and I had to speak my mind.

LETICIA: Young people get harassed by the police, from the Community Support Officers and now from the Challenge Walkers.

IONA: We are trying to get de board to elp with equipment for the yout activities so dat de young people can gather again. Dey just staying up all night on the computer and den sleeping all day till late!

NARRATOR: I now had a possible explanation as to why the local area was so empty that morning.

MARY: What is there for them to do? Look how long it is taking this centre to get set up?

IONA: Back ome der was so much church gaderings going on – one after de oder.

LETICIA: What can they learn from church gatherings?

IONA: So playing pool gathering is any better?

Her question is ignored.

INTERVIEWER: So, what do you think you have gained from learning on the course?

DOROTHY: We can challenge the men now.

Everyone laughs.

ALL: Challenge them! Yes!

The women are now speaking all at once again. They are repeating themselves and contest each other's examples of ways to challenge the male-dominated Challenge board meetings.

SCENE 5: A voice at board meetings

INTERVIEWER: And what about the benefits of your learning for others in the community?

YVONNE: I feel better equipped to serve the community.

INTERVIEWER: And this is as a result of your new skills?

IONA: Everybody jus showing off and Dorothy asking some detective questions.

JUNE: She was good, really good. What a bacchanal at the Regeneration Board!

The women are laughing and speaking over each other. They are confirming June's assertion.

LETICIA: Oh yes. She was good.

INTERVIEWER: What type of questions were these?

IONA: Well she did her homework and she never let im get away with anyting.

INTERVIEWER: Him?

DOROTHY: Steve Black from the Housing Office of course. That man is so crafty.

MARY: He does not like to spend one penny for the area and it is not even his money.

INTERVIEWER: So what questions did you ask, Dorothy?

DOROTHY: About why Martha had to die in that place, alone? And why it took the housing people so long to find her? And about how they had to mash up all the nice furniture she had inside there when people in the community could have well done with those tables and chairs. The people are so wicked. Martha had some nice things in her place.

MARY: That done now. The furniture is not important now but she should not have had to go that way. That is why what we are doing in the group is so very important.

IONA: And we cannot keep going back. We ave to move forward.

INTERVIEWER: So tell me more about the learning from the course. How does it help you on an individual level?

YVONNE: It helped with confidence-building. Tatiana kept telling us how it is important to gather facts – not just come up there and ask stupid questions. I did not ask questions before because I did not have any facts. Now we all come to the meetings prepared with at least one question to ask.

DOROTHY: And you know what? These people afraid of us now! We turn too bright!

MARY: They look like they fear us for true.

The women laugh. They are all talking at once and repeating each other's words.

NARRATOR: I was curious about the fragments of this story that they had begun to share but decided to let it emerge later.

IONA: *(laughing)* Dem soon kick us out!

LETICIA: You know it is Dorothy, Yvonne and Mary who are officially on the board but they let the rest of us attend as we are from the community and they cannot stop us.

MARY: You know, they don't know who is who.

Everyone laughs.

LETICIA: But we cannot vote.

Everyone laughs.

SCENE 6: *In action at the board meeting*

DOROTHY: Imagine that, when I first come to this country I was just a shy young girl with no education but now every week I am getting plenty papers this high to read!

MARY: And you are writing speeches for the meetings!

DOROTHY: And I am enjoying every minute of it.

LETICIA: You know that Dorothy is the only one that can get away with a full five minutes' speech in a one-minute slot! That is supposed to be to ask a question and make a brief point!

DOROTHY: I work hard on these speeches and I rehearse them but you know when you have the speech and you giving the speech and you look around you and you have to pause and pause again, and then take a breath, and then relax yourself before you continue.

Everyone laughs.

MARY: So why do you have to look around so much – just read your speech woman!

DOROTHY: You don't remember. Tatiana tell we must give eye contact!

LETICIA: Yes but only for second or two. You cannot keep looking people up and down. Over and over again!

IONA: And you mus not look at people over de top of your glasses! You can give that Mr Chamberlain some bad looks. You must stop dat because it is rude.

DOROTHY: But the man can look so mash up and untidy. How can the man come to these meetings looking so bad?

Everyone laughs.

IONA: Him look renk for true.

INTERVIEWER: In what other ways did the course help you?

MARY: It helped us to listen and be ready to respond to what they tell us. Before we were just so relieved to put the question that we didn't bother listen to the reply!

Incessant laughing.

MARY: But now we fire back!

ALL: *(laughing and repeating)* We fire back!

YVONNE: Even if Dorothy not getting it right she still fire back!

LETICIA: She just challenges everything.

JUNE: Her standard line is: 'That is unacceptable!'

Everyone laughs.

IONA: We don't want dem to tink we are foolish – dat is what the course is teaching us – to listen, tink before speaking and support each other. It is teaching us not to just rush into tings – but take a moment to confer with each other. We see dem doing it all de while at de town all.

LETICIA: We just have two more sessions left and we have to bring the teacher our feedback, questions and reflections from the meetings.

INTERVIEWER: By the teacher you mean the trainer?

LETICIA: Yes of course.

INTERVIEWER: So the course is teaching you a great deal would you say?

LETICIA: Just *so* much but the time just fly by and the first session was not easy because we had to do so much talking. And the reading was hard as we were forced to read the reports.

DOROTHY: Some of us just read the minutes and the agenda.

INTERVIEWER: So you can see some interesting progress along the way?

MARY: Yes because we are all learning and improving as we go along and Tatiana is good at encouraging us; she makes us feel better about succeeding and feeling good. Like what we are doing is important and worthwhile.

LETICIA: I came over as a child and I remember primary school being very much like fun. Back home they were really strict about education and suddenly here – it's all fun. I realized now that in some subjects, I knew all the answers and was very good at writing, spelling and grammar compared to the other children in class. But at that time I used to get a lot of racist abuse from the other children so I became very quiet and didn't say much for a long time until my English teacher gave me encouraging comments about my essay and that really motivated me to write more and learn more.

SCENE 7: Rebelling at the board meeting

INTERVIEWER: Is there anything else you would like to be learning apart from the skills for effective committee participation?

IONA: How to get more money for what we are doing.

INTERVIEWER: You mean for the work you are doing in the group?

IONA: Yes for our work with de isolated people dem in the blocks.

MARY: We need to know how to apply for grants because we want more women to join us from the community and we need money to receive more so more women can take part in things.

IONA: We don't want everyone to jus walk all over us. Did you see ow dat woman from Debden Block get robbed the udda day? And she was right der inside er flat, in broad daylight. They know what dey are doing – dey jus watch. We want de surveillance back on dat side but dey keep saying no money. But every flat in Judit Latymer block is already covered!

INTERVIEWER: Judith Latymer?

MARY: She is on the board and also on the council.

YVONNE: Powerful.

DOROTHY: But she is a decent woman and we all want to help each other.

IONA: You change your tune Dorothy. It's like you seem to like everybody nowadays.

Everyone laughs.

DOROTHY: But you know I have a very important role and I am responsible and have to be seen to be respectful.

SCENE 8: Missed education

INTERVIEWER: Do you take part in any other learning at any other centre?

JUNE: I was doing an access course at the college at one time when my children were younger but I had so much trouble with them that I had to give it up.

DOROTHY: And she have girls you know. Not boys. Girls should not give trouble.

IONA: These days de girls are just as bad.

YVONNE: It is a real struggle when you are on your own with children.

JUNE: I wanted to go to university but left school with nothing really.

DOROTHY: Left school!

JUNE: OK I had problems with the other children and had to fight racism and could not learn but I want to study now – I did not want to at that time but now I think different.

MARY: You were bad and you expect your children not to be bad like you.

LETICIA: Don't be hard on her. Those days were tough for us.

NARRATOR: The older women appear to think that the younger members of the group had a better chance of access to education but, as these comments indicate, some of the first-generation African Caribbean women who arrived as young children clearly faced racism in the school system.

DOROTHY: But you three children *(referring to YVONNE, JUNE and LETICIA)* don't know what the word 'tough' is – not like us. You all get the chance for a good education and plenty of good teachers. Back home, we just get the chance with one teacher who had to teach the whole village!

Laughter.

IONA: That is not true, Dorothy. His wife used to teach us too.

Everyone laughs.

Review of Act 4

While the previous act dealt with informal learning taking place outside a dedicated learning environment (McGivney, 1999), this act focused on the type of learning that 'occupies a middle position between learning that is an incidental by-product of other activities (informal learning) and intentional instructional (formal learning)' (Field, 2006a: 53). Act 4 depicted non-formal learning in the community – the organized learning that takes place largely in local community centres and invariably with the individuals completing courses, though often with no formal certificates at the end of the process. However, a great deal of benefit is accrued from this approach, not just for the individual but, as suggested in the previous act, for the wider community.

In this last act the women present a performance-style learning face. They appear to be asking stage-managed questions and delivering their speeches to full effect on the Challenge board. Here the women are very aware of their audience: one woman states 'everybody showing off and Dorothy asking some detective questions'. Dorothy herself is flamboyant in her delivery and aware of her audience as she takes her time to deliver her carefully prepared contribution. I reflect on the fact that she has expressed a quiet but clear endorsement of Judith Latymer, the 'opposition' councillor, and wonder whether this might be a case of silencing the voices of the rebels through their incorporation. Has the course assisted in marginalizing the women's voices or is there still a balance of challenging voices? I concluded that in the polyrhythmic nature of their social interaction, the women would at some point be able to assess the limits and strengths of their role on the Challenge board.

Chapter 5

In search of our carnival spirits

ACT 5: Support for sisters in the inner city: A story of community courage

CAST OF CHARACTERS

NARRATOR	INTERVIEWER speaks to the audience, as an aside
INTERVIEWER	Speaks directly to the characters
RASHIDA	Aged 72, from Trinidad
SELENA	Aged 74, from Guyana
INEZ	Aged 53, from Barbados; coordinator/chairperson
BARBARA	Aged 59, from Grenada
BETTY	Aged 62, from St Kitts; community volunteer – elders' group
THERESA	Aged 75, from Trinidad
AUDREY	Aged 56, from Nevis
AMRU	Male character; founder of Heritage Centre

SCENE 1: Approaching the Hanston Heritage Centre

It is just before midday and the INTERVIEWER is walking down a narrow road in Hanston City Centre. Halfway down the road of three tiered terraced houses, she cuts across another narrow road and arrives at a corner house with large curtainless bay windows. There is a variety of African artwork and a large sign reads: 'The Hanston Community Arts Project'. In the next window of the ground floor, there is a photograph of the Ethiopian Emperor, Haile Selassie, beside a bright red, green and gold sign bearing the words 'Hanston Heritage Centre'.

SCENE 2: An anxious but warm welcome

A dreadlocked middle-aged man with spectacles is holding on tightly to a large number of assorted letters. He opens the door to the Hanston Heritage Centre. It appears that he may have just arrived at the centre and is now busy opening the mail.

AMRU: *(in a serious, slightly angry tone)* Good afternoon. *(shouts)* Inez! Betty! *(turns to INTERVIEWER)* You must be the lady doing the research. *(does not wait for a reply)* They are through there but wait in here.

AMRU speaks firmly to the interviewer as he escorts her to an open-plan area, which clearly served as a front room but is now a training room.

Near the entrance to the main door is a computer and a large wooden table laden with red tea cups and saucers and surrounded by faded copies of the West Indian People. The front pages of the newspapers display the faces of black youths under a large caption reading: 'Not another drop!' In the middle of the room there are some red sofas around a coffee table. Toward the far end of the room are several computers. A teenage girl wearing headphones is using one of them.

AMRU: *(pointing the INTERVIEWER to the red sofas)* Take a seat. I will get out of your way shortly. *(begins to rummage through papers in a small filing cabinet near the large table and then mutters under his breath)* I hope they tell you this is their last meeting here.

Before the INTERVIEWER has an opportunity to sit down, the chattering voices of women can be heard in the hallway and she catches sight of distinctly colourful African Caribbean costumes, as a group of women enter the room one by one.

AUDREY: *(an older dark-skinned woman wearing a green African wrap dress)* Hello dear, we are just making some tea. Would you like a cup?

A woman in red, RASHIDA, smiles at the INTERVIEWER.

INEZ: *(a tall, slim woman, wearing a smart bright yellow and royal blue gown)* Hello, I am Inez – it is good to see the person I have been talking to over the telephone. *(she holds out her hands to the INTERVIEWER)*

INTERVIEWER: *(speaking to a third woman)* Hello Betty.

The INTERVIEWER recognizes the dreadlocked Betty from her photograph in the Heritage Centre brochure.

BETTY: Hello. Let me introduce you to my sisters.

RASHIDA: *(of Caribbean Indian descent, she holds out her hands to the INTERVIEWER and speaks with a strong Trinidadian accent)* I am Rashida, good to meet you.

SCENE 3: *Roles, learning and community expectations*

The women gather around the interviewer on the sofas in the centre of the room, ignoring the man and responding comfortably to the INTERVIEWER's questions. She had not expected such a large turnout. The women are smartly dressed as if for an occasion, and she wonders whether they have dressed especially for the interview.

INTERVIEWER: So, what are your roles here?

INEZ: I am a volunteer with the group. I help with the Caribbean history room upstairs. I do administration, answer the telephone and I am a student on the ICT course.

SELENA: I am one of the volunteers for the Black Mother's Survival project and I come here for the ICT skills classes for women.

BARBARA: I help the tutor with the Information, Communications and Technologies course here on Monday afternoons. I gained my qualifications from Hanston College.

INTERVIEWER: *(wondering why BARBARA feels the need to tell where her qualifications came from)* Thank you, Barbara.

BARBARA: *(moving closer to the INTERVIEWER and whispering)* Amru thinks we are wasting money bringing in Frontline to deliver the training and that we in the community can do it just as well – but they train the council staff and they are real experts.

BARBARA looks back at AMRU, who is still in the room and appearing to look busy. The INTERVIEWER hears the muffled words from the openly disgruntled man.

AMRU: *(mumbling)* When are they going to learn … Eurocentric … Nonsense.

SELENA: *(loudly)* We learn far better from the experts and we are more motivated to learning when we are taught by them.

BETTY: And we want to continue the ICT training here because that way Amru would be able to keep running the centre and he could show that good work was still going on. But women are always prioritized these days and sometimes I think men have to work harder for things.

INEZ: You must be joking!

The women are now talking loudly all at once, in disapproval of BETTY's statement.

NARRATOR: I observed that Betty is quiet and smiling and I suspect she is being deliberately provocative.

AMRU: *(not joining in the conversation but muttering and repeating)* Thirty years in the community! Thirty years in the community!

AMRU finally leaves the room.

INEZ: *(speaking slowly and seriously as she looks at the INTERVIEWER)* That is my husband but we are not getting along at all.

RASHIDA: The man work hard for true and how all you can disrespect him so?

INEZ ignores the question, which she knows is meant for her.

Image and text courtesy of Looshan Saltfish

Figure 6: Mavista – 'Learning is talking history. We have to pass it on – good or bad'

SCENE 4: Skills for supporting community

SELENA: Yes, the man work very hard for true.

THERESA: Yes, you cannot deny that. It is hard to find a man who can work so hard for the community.

The women ignore the statement and are now debating whether women's projects are given priority and they move back and forth from what appears to be angry confrontations but with moments of loud laughter.

THERESA: The man is a stalwart of the community!

AUDREY: He has his supporters in the community.

BARBARA: Everything is about supporting women right now.

INEZ: That is what is killing him.

SELENA: You can't tell him that.

THERESA: But the Heritage Centre is the heart of our community!

AUDREY: Whose side are you on?

Everyone laughs.

BETTY: You have to give him credit for all that work with the youths.

AUDREY: So who works harder than Inez?

BARBARA: Yes, tell us!

All the women are talking at the same time and the INTERVIEWER decides to intervene so as to change the focus of the discussion.

INTERVIEWER: So you are all volunteers for the project, but first tell me about the training.

The women are all silent for a moment as they think about their response to the INTERVIEWERS's question.

AUDREY: The training is an information communication course that is teaching us how to improve our typing skills using [Microsoft®] Word so we are learning to develop our computer skills, but the course is also showing us how to use the Internet and how to prepare emails. We cannot afford to pay for this sort of thing so for us the centre is invaluable.

SELENA: We are taking the ICT course to help improve our knowledge and skills.

INEZ: We are building together the material for the website for our project because we want local women to know more about our work. We have a little genius here – my granddaughter who is helping with our website. She is setting us up a Facebook website.

INEZ looks behind her at the young woman who is using the computer at the far end of the room.

AUDREY: The computer classes help with networking and keeping us in contact with other black mothers because through email we can stay in touch. Most of us had to stop our training to raise children. Now we get a second chance.

INTERVIEWER: How does the training help you, Theresa?

THERESA: I am 75 – no more young children to look after. My great-grandchild is big now. I am in good health and have survived breast cancer and two muggers and now I have a computer at home and a mobile phone. I am a survivor and I feel a very happy woman!

Everyone nods and laughs.

INTERVIEWER: And what about you, Rashida?

RASHIDA: A lot of us need to get skills for interacting with others and the city officials. Before I came here I was going to the library to learn computer skills but they cut back on the library opening times now and the one day I could go, the library is closed. On the other days the place is pack up with young people using the computers. There is a whole library full up with books but all they want to do is gather round the computer.

SELENA: They come in straight after school and there is no computer to use and I cannot understand the system to book it and sometimes you have to wait so long and I just get fed up and leave.

THERESA: The library workers are very helpful. Before I had my computer, I would go there and they would sit by the computer with me and give me one-to-one tuition – but you have to book for that. You have to be very patient to do this job but I find all the library workers seem to enjoy their work. They are very patient. At the Grove Library they have no time for you.

AUDREY: But these days after the first hour in the library you have to pay to use the computers.

INTERVIEWER: So it is much more convenient to learn here at the centre?

RASHIDA: Of course, because we have no problems getting to use the computer!

INEZ: If only Amru had more patience with us.

SCENE 5: Engaging with lifelong learning

INTERVIEWER: What does lifelong learning mean to you?

SELENA: Lifelong – it never stops!

INEZ: I have always had a worry about learning. I feel fearful that because I just have the basic qualification from school that I cannot move on because of it. It is like I have the qualification that young children have and for that reason I have never had the confidence to apply for the youth work diploma. My husband has that qualification but he also has O levels and all other types of qualifications too. To me lifelong learning is about helping yourself but also about learning together with others. We need motivation when we get to our age.

THERESA: I came to England in 1956 and it cost me $390 Trinidadian dollars and 60 cents to get here. The journey took us six weeks. I was 23 and a bit shy, but when you are on a big ship with plenty people for that length of time, you learn to mix. That was lifelong learning for me! When I landed, as big as I was, I wanted an education, but there was no money for learning. I had to find work straight away.

RASHIDA: There was never any money for learning and I missed out on proper education when I was young. That is why we have lifelong learning to be able to do it when we can today. To me you can never feel satisfied without education. You just feel something is missing and you have to strive for it.

SELENA: Lifelong learning is having the courage to continue learning at a mature age.

RASHIDA: It is a second chance to learn – no more joyful times but just hard times with the children – time for me now. And when the council cannot help some of us can rely on the immediate family or the extended family.

BETTY: Having a base here makes things possible for us. We are free to be ourselves and can chastise each other without the children hearing us carry on a way! *(she looks over at the teenager with the headphones)*

Laughter.

BETTY: How she can work with that blasted noise in her ears?!

More laughter.

INTERVIEWER: What does lifelong learning mean to you, Barbara?

BARBARA: Lifelong learning is the learning that is acquired in a whole lifetime and passed on to others – like Anancy stories.

NARRATOR: A number of lifelong learning themes are apparent in this scene, including ideas of time, place and how the women understood the concept of learning. Barriers to learning through life also emerged, including lack of money, inadequate facilities and women's competing priorities, notably stopping learning to care for children. The value of community organizations in offering second-chance opportunities to learn contributed to my reflections on how the women understood the nature of lifelong learning.

SCENE 6: *Reflecting on black youth*

INTERVIEWER: Tell me about the work of your group.

AUDREY: We are a Black Mothers' survival project and work below the radar. We run a support group for mothers who have experienced trauma or violence, mostly involving their children. We put a little money together ourselves but no one have money these days. We can hardly put anything decent in the church collection box anymore. The women don't come to us seeking professional advice. We reach out to them giving sisterly support to talk things through. So many of us have the same experiences and we think our support is already raising the self-esteem of the mothers we come into contact with.

The women re-assert similar statements for the benefit of the INTERVIEWER.

RASHIDA: We hear things in church and we network with black mothers experiencing the same thing and we work to give them courage to deal with their situation. It is always a very frightening experience when you get that knock on the door from the police about your son or daughter.

BARBARA: For young people, not learning and not being in school is a problem because when you are learning you do not get yourself into trouble.

THERESA: If only the school could keep them in there. That is where the problem lies. The schools are not tough enough with young people and they get involved in crime. The discipline we had back home in Trinidad was a regime and you had to respect that regime.

SELENA: But not only in Trinidad.

BETTY: All over the Caribbean.

SELENA: My great-grandson nearly got locked up but lucky he was underage and he was doing so well in the school but somehow he just got lost and no longer interested in his schoolwork. There are just not enough mentors to stick with them and come talk to them when they are having problems. Sometimes a mother's love is just not enough.

NARRATOR: The question on the work of their group seems to have morphed into what's wrong with schooling, young people and crime.

BETTY: But today we experience much worse than prison; young people are dying on the streets and mothers have to carry on.

INEZ: We always say that we are lucky we had a girl child and our girl child produced another girl grandchild for us. Not saying that we don't know about the girl gangs but, compared to boys, girls are less trouble when it comes to the police and crime.

BARBARA: You are so fortunate.

INEZ ignores the statement.

AUDREY: My grandson and his bad friends were in a gang and us as mothers, we feel powerless to do anything. We try so hard but we are constantly losing control of things and we need the support of other women as we are mostly on our own.

INEZ: We are tired and exhausted and so what else can we do but support each other?

BETTY: There are parts of Hanston that has had its fair share of problems and not all the women have support. We are grandmothers, great-grandmothers and mothers losing children in the same way and we have to go on. There is no escape.

AUDREY: Some of us get messed up ourselves.

INEZ: We have had some really dreadful things happen in our area. *(looks enquiringly at the INTERVIEWER)*

BARBARA: You can get very depressed even though there is nothing you can do about it. You fight with them and sometimes even want to call the police on them but that is your child. You cannot do that.

There is silence for a moment.

SCENE 7: *Supporting black mothers in the community*

INTERVIEWER: And what type of support is it that you provide?

BARBARA: We bring cake and we talk. Where we can, we put the mothers in touch with experts who can help.

RASHIDA: And you know I cannot bring myself to get emotional – not when I am supporting the women.

NARRATOR: It is interesting how Rashida acknowledges her 'professional' role … even though emotions clearly emerge around these issues.

SELENA: Sometimes talking is enough. We find out what can be done. We don't put leaflets about. It is just word of mouth.

RASHIDA: We are just there for giving the women support and we put the women in touch with other women going through the same thing, and sometimes the law centre and the councillors.

The women repeat their mission.

BETTY: So many of the black mothers affected feel like giving up and don't really know their rights. Many blame themselves for the crimes inflicted by their children on others – or for the crimes which are committed on their children.

SELENA: And of course it is their fault mostly.

INTERVIEWER: What do you mean?

SELENA: Sad to say, it is the way these young women raise their boys.

BARBARA: How can you say that?

AUDREY: Like you don't know the pressure black mothers are under nowadays.

RASHIDA: But she is only speaking the truth.

All the women are now talking quickly and all at once. The INTERVIEWER is ignored.

NARRATOR: Selena's statement has caused much anxiety. I observe the women for a few moments speaking to, and at, each other in their various Caribbean dialects. There are no moments of laughter.

There is silence from the women.

INEZ: *(breaking the silence)* I was only blessed with one child.

All the women laugh.

INEZ: But it was no easy ride.

More laughter.

BARBARA: And you had constant help from your man.

Laughter.

THERESA: Back home young people had nothing. Children now have everything …

AUDREY: Stop that now.

There is another lull in the conversation.

INEZ: *(speaking in a quiet voice)* Everyone is entitled to their own opinion but we don't always listen to each other. We want to start a blog for grandmothers because most of the mothers these days are children themselves. As grandmothers and great-grandmothers we don't talk with each other enough. We can do a lot more in our community to support each other. We tend to keep ourselves to ourselves and think that in the area, it is only our family who are going through this type of trouble.

THERESA: My great-grandson was incarcerated when he was only 16. A young offender and he used to get vex up quick.

The women all peer at THERESA for a while.

BETTY: *(seeming to feel the need to re-state the work of the project again)* We are doing different things in the community but the main thing is talking with others. We run the support group for mothers who have been experiencing emotional pain because of crime carried out by their children on others or crime perpetrated on their children by others. When your child commits a crime it is a very personal thing and most mothers feel ashamed and want to keep themselves to themselves. We find grandmothers show a lot more courage and want to come out to give support to the project when they can – when they are not looking after children. Some blame their children, others blame the schools but it is the society – the world we live in today – that is to blame.

NARRATOR: This seemed a very important project and the women tended to understate the significance of their involvement.

INEZ: My husband *(she looks behind her to check that he is not in the room)* thinks as women we just give out too much information about our work. We have been looking to get our project funding and it looks like it's coming through now but other projects lost their funding – like his. There is no money to fund the Heritage Centre and he is hopping mad – so we might soon need to find a new venue for our work! *(she laughs out loud in a disappointed way and then stops abruptly)*

INTERVIEWER: *(remembering the words of AMRU, the male worker)* And how long are you here for?

INEZ: Well I know we don't need to go anywhere for now. This centre will be here for some time but why fund our work and not fund the centre? It does not make sense. There is talk of the women's issues being given priority or maybe because it seen as a one-off – small money. But we in the community are our worst enemies as we do not talk to each other. We don't. *(speaks slowly, quietly but assertively)* Not even husbands and wives talk.

BETTY: That's the trouble with our community.

AUDREY: No togetherness!

THERESA: None whatsoever!

INEZ: *(loudly)* Not even husbands and wives talk!

BETTY: You said that already!

Everyone laughs. Then the women are talking over each other, repeating and stressing each other's words. AMRU returns. He enters through a door at the back of the room and moves across to the large desk near the front windows. He appears to want to intervene in the conversation again. However, the women ignore him and carry on with their banter.

NARRATOR: I asked myself whether loss of funding for community centres and closure of projects meant the end of this type of informal learning, social networking and community support.

SCENE 8: The wider benefits of learning

INTERVIEWER: What are the benefits of your learning? And how are you passing on your learning?

BARBARA: I have continued to struggle and have had an education but have still taken every short course that I could get my hands on because you can never learn enough. It is about giving and receiving.

INTERVIEWER: Explain that a little more.

BARBARA: I believe I have been able to pass my learning on to others by the volunteering work that I have done. I have been able to manage to survive the education system. I have not learnt very much through it as a result of my own efforts and struggles within it and against it. But I have definitely been able to share my particular experiences and I feel over the years others have benefited from it, but I want to develop my knowledge and skills further in order to move into more higher education.

NARRATOR: Barbara's statement provoked a great deal of thought, knitting together multiple ideas around barriers, surviving and thriving within learning systems.

INTERVIEWER: So how much is your learning on the ICT course benefiting you and how is it helping with your work in the community?

THERESA: *(speaking as if this is what the INTERVIEWER expects to hear)* The learning is benefiting because we are learning to type and learning to spell and we can communicate more effectively.

SELENA: And we can communicate with family and friends and send photographs via the net and more women can join us.

At that moment, the doorbell rings loudly.

INEZ: *(rushing out to open the front door)* He is here.

BETTY: But he is well early.

A loud male voice is heard coming from the corridor: 'All dressed up and ready ladies?' The women look very excited and anxious and all get up hurriedly and begin to attend to their attire.

BARBARA: The photographer from the newspaper is here. We are having a group photograph for our project launch.

NARRATOR: I had not been told that the women were expecting to be photographed and now I understood why they had all turned up and were all wearing traditional dress. The ways in which I had learnt what was happening or what was being referred to by various women gradually and in fragments reminded me of Gubrium and Holstein's advice that the empirical material here was 'not simply stories, as if they were self-evident texts with plots, themes, points, beginnings, middles, and ends' (Gubrium and Holstein, 2001: xvii). Although these were present 'in the production, communication, and appreciation of accounts' (ibid.) my role was to reassemble fragments and make sense of their narratives.

I looked over at the group of women fussing over their appearance as they considered the achievements of their project. I could not help feeling a sense of pride, as for me they had accomplished something inspiring.

ACT 6: Playing Mas: A story of learning for the promotion of Caribbean heritage

This act presents the story of non-formal learning from eight members of the West Grove Park Carnival Group.

CAST OF CHARACTERS

NARRATOR	The INTERVIEWER speaks to the audience, as an aside
INTERVIEWER	Speaks directly to the characters
BRENDA	Aged 65, from Trinidad
MERLINA	Aged 67, from Trinidad
ANNE-MARIE	Aged 75, from Barbados
BEATRICE	Aged 54, from St Vincent
EVONNE	Aged 59, from Guyana
MAXINE	Aged 55, from Trinidad
MINDY	Aged 76, from Trinidad
ANNIE	Aged 53, from Barbados

SCENE 1: *Approaching the Hibiscus Centre*

The INTERVIEWER is on a gloomy high street gazing up at an old gym building above a takeaway. The Hibiscus Centre building is located above a discount pound shop and sits in between two popular chain betting shops. On hearing the buzzer released, the INTERVIEWER takes the short flight of stairs to the first floor. The words in the Calypso melody echo loudly: 'Walk and wine ... Walk and wine ...'

SCENE 2: *Inside the Hibiscus Centre*

The INTERVIEWER enters a bright space ablaze with colour – emerald greens, cadmium reds – and there is a large, bright, multicoloured mural on the wall. The scene is a dramatic contrast to the dreariness of the high street. Next to the mural is a large framed certificate with the words: 'Best Costume 2005'. The room is reminiscent of a modern purpose-built warehouse. Noisy talkative women sit around laden tables. Their hands are full of coloured cloths as they skilfully sew and weave in tandem. Loud music of a carnival kind plays in the background.

SCENE 3: *Welcome to our carnival group*

The women introduce themselves to the INTERVIEWER *and return to their conversation. One woman addresses the interviewer.*

ANNE-MARIE: We are not working today. We are only gathering to meet with you. But as you can see, the work continues.

ANNIE: Working? Most of us just come here for a laugh.

The music in the background changes to: 'Get something and wave! Get something and wave!'

MERLINA: Just to make commess and bacchanal in the place.

MAXINE: *(speaking sternly)* When there is plenty work to do.

MINDY: *(in a serious tone)* You young people can learn so much if you take more pride in what you doing.

MERLINA: *(laughing)* Keep the bacchanal and spirit of carnival alive.

MINDY: It is not about liming and having a good time for good time sake.

EVONNE: We only have one tradition.

BEATRICE: And that is carnival.

BRENDA: Too right.

ANNE-MARIE: And what about our music?

MERLINA: And our food. 'Doubles!'

MAXINE: Buss up Shut!

MINDY: Gimmee the roti!

ANNE-MARIE: And what about de 'Cou Cou and flying fish!'

The women are now all laughing.

ANNIE: *(laughing and shaking her head)* We just watch.

SCENE 4: *Group Interview*

MINDY: I am a seamstress. Qualified and experienced.

The other women laugh.

ANNIE: There are no more seamstresses, Mindy.

NARRATOR: The more mature women in the group are trying to portray a serious and weighty side to the activity of creating carnival costumes. The younger women appear not to be appreciative of the advice of the older women instructors.

MINDY: *(speaking with a strong Trinidadian accent)* I am incensed when I hear this. A seamstress is a very important role. My mother and her mother and probably her mother before her was a seamstress.

BEATRICE: You going back well far now.

NARRATOR: Most of the women are now laughing, but one woman speaks in support of Mindy.

ANNE-MARIE: (speaking with a high-pitched Bajan accent) All too right, tell them Mindy.

NARRATOR: I decided these exchanges, interesting as they were, needed some guiding toward the purpose of my visit.

INTERVIEWER: What do you all understand by the term 'lifelong learning'?

MERLINA: Freedom! Total freedom to learn when you want.

BEATRICE: And what you want.

MINDY: No, not what you want.

BRENDA: You think I could study for a degree?

INTERVIEWER: Why not?

MERLINA: Of course you can.

NARRATOR: The women begin to speak all at once at each other in strong patois with serious overtones. I can hear comments about who can and who cannot study for a degree, how smart they need to be to study for a degree, how they cannot afford to study anyway, what funding was necessary for a degree, how they missed out on education and how things could have been different for them. I considered my own journey and desire for education and how social networks had played a major role in helping me realize particular goals.

SCENE 5: Concentrating on learning

The INTERVIEWER interrupts the conversations.

INTERVIEWER: And how are you learning in this wonderful space?

ANNIE: I would like to study costume design

The INTERVIEWER's specific question is ignored.

ANNIE: At art school.

MINDY: But what do you think you doing now?

ANNIE: This not at a specialist trade.

MINDY: Specialist trade!

ANNE-MARIE: Are you kidding me!

ANNIE: I mean fashion, at a college. You do so much sophisticated formal stuff there.

MERLINA: All this time you spent sky-larking. Is only now you thinking of that?!

ANNE-MARIE: Well I hope you put this training you getting here to good use.

MINDY: Good luck to you! You ungrateful madam! *(throws her sewing in the air)*

ANNIE: What I am doing here will help – but I want a recognized qualification! *(appears not to believe that the type of learning occurring at the centre has any real value)*

BRENDA: If you want a Hibiscus certificate, you know you will get one.

ANNIE rolls her eyes.

EVONNE: I got my certificate last year and it is up on my wall.

ANNIE: Yes I know.

BEATRICE: But you want a first-class certificate!

EVONNE: I demonstrated that I could design, cut and sew.

MAXINE: You won't convince that one. I don't know why we even bother with her! Just like these layabout young people. They don't know how good they have it!

ANNE-MARIE: *(attempting to lighten the mood)* Some of you want to make the costumes and some of you just want to wear it, jump up and down in it. You want to win the prizes but you all don't know how lucky you are!

MINDY: Some of you want to catch man in that costume too!

Everyone laughs.

BRENDA: These young women gone to town with the winding, giving our islands a bad reputation.

ANNIE: They get on worse in Trin'dad.

BEATRICE: Me is not from Trinidad.

ANNIE: Well in St Vincent too I am sure.

Everyone laughs. BRENDA moves to the sound of the taped music: 'They say I too young to soca ... They say I too young to soca ...' MINDY demonstrates a 'wine' (sensuous dance). 'They say I too young to soca!' More laughing.

SCENE 6: *Learning and playing mas*

INTERVIEWER: So Merlina, would you say you are learning here?

MERLINA: Certainly – and the learning is good when you have time on your hands and nothing on your mind.

ANNIE: Just make sure you have that needle on your mind before you juke out me eye!

Everyone laughs.

MERLINA: Don't worry I know where this needle going. How many years I am sewing like this!

INTERVIEWER: So about learning ...

MERLINA: The girls are not learning – they just playing mas right here inside the place – learning about other people's business – sure!

Everyone laughs. The younger women giggle.

BRENDA: But you can talk, Merlina – we hear it all the scandal from you!

MINDY: I don't know what is wrong with Anancy stories but no, you all just want to hear about pure rudeness.

More laughter.

Image and text courtesy of Steve Ecco

Figure 7: Learning Matriarchs – 'What story you coming to learn about from Mama Mamaguise today?'

INTERVIEWER: This centre looks like it serves a really good purpose?

BRENDA: We work on things all year round. We get a grant from the council and we have people coming in to show us the new designs and tricks of the trade. Now we are teaching others our own designs.

Review of Act 6

The women in Act 6 appeared as a group that was very open to outsiders but, compared to earlier acts, less able to focus on what they understood by learning, except in a few cases. I reflected on what the women were doing at the centre and how they understood their activities. One woman (Mindy) had pointed out that the younger women could 'learn so much' from the centre. However, it appeared that the majority of the women did not see the Hibiscus Centre as a centre for learning. When asked about how she was learning at the centre, Annie ignored the question and declared: 'I would like to study costume design.' She referred to what the women were involved in at the centre as 'not a specialist trade like fashion at a college'. Merlina, however, was more focused and serious about lifelong learning and said that it offered 'total freedom to learn when you want'. Unlike most of the others, for her it connected what she was doing at the centre with learning. But for the majority, it appeared that learning was perceived as formal and serious and taking place in a college setting and not in the form of social participation in the way they were demonstrating at the Hibiscus Centre.

Conclusion

This chapter reflects two different faces of learning: that relating to developing skills to assist others in the community, and that relating to, as many would see it, pursuing more personal interests. The common thread they share is the eagerness with which the women prepare for their respective 'performances' that emerge from the learning, whether this involves donning Caribbean outfits in readiness for a press photographer, rehearsing speeches or content for meetings or preparing costumes for a forthcoming entertainment event. The women appear to remember carnival and their oral history back home in the Caribbean. In the acts, we see the women engage in dramatics as they discuss their learning, and some dress in Caribbean costume. And they laugh constantly, typifying their happy Caribbean carnival spirit. In the second act, the women engage in serious discussion but wear colourful Caribbean costume and present a Caribbean carnival image as they prepare for the photograph for the local newspaper, which will be read in the wider community.

In Act 1 the women are directly focused on learning and helping the wider community with their learning, but focused too on maximizing their learning to enhance their own opportunities. On the other hand, some of the women in Act 6 appear not to be altogether focused on learning but rather on self and amusement, unlike the vast majority of women in the stories so far. All the acts in this chapter encompass a search for something lost; a woman in Act 6 captures this when she says: 'Keep the spirit of carnival alive.'

Chapter 6

Spreading our wings

Stories of learning in a British education system

ACT 7: Slackness and toughness in the British education system: A story of mentoring for community

The three women volunteers are all members of the Black Learners and Achievers Project (BLAP) and act as mentors to children who attend local primary and secondary schools and come to the project for extra mathematics and English classes. The home of BLAP is a small supplementary teaching classroom located beyond the kitchen of the Lincolnvale Caribbean Community bakery, situated on the edge of the city centre.

CAST OF CHARACTERS

NARRATOR	The INTERVIEWER speaks to the audience, as an aside
INTERVIEWER	Speaks directly to the characters
ELDRA	Aged 70, from St Vincent; came to the UK in 1959, aged 20 **College course:** Explorers Diploma for Older Learners **Mode:** 16 weeks full-time residential **College:** Hillviewdale Further Education College **Vocation:** Former carer/former project manager with a black project/former local councillor
VEREEN	Aged 52, from Grenada; came to the UK in 1958, aged 2 **College course:** Teacher training **Mode:** Full-time: three days a week. **College:** Lincolnvale Community College **Vocation:** Former library worker/former teaching assistant /former carer

CANDACE	Aged 54, from Jamaica; came to the UK in 1959, aged 5
	College course: Access to Higher Education
	Mode: Part-time: one evening a week
	College: Highfield Adult Learning College
	Vocation: Former community worker/former short-life housing manager

SCENE 1: *Setting the scene*

The group interview with the three women is followed by a one-to-one interview with ELDRA, the eldest in the group. The interview begins amidst the aroma of freshly baked hard-dough breads, fried dumplings and patties, which are on display on the warming trays in the kitchen. It is Saturday morning and the shop is preparing for its Saturday morning customers.

BAKER 1: More carrot juice please, Ms Vilma.

BAKER 2: You all, mind the pot on the fire!

SCENE 2: *Welcome*

ELDRA: *(in a loud and authoritative voice)* Welcome to the Black Learners and Achievers Project.

INTERVIEWER: Hello. I am very pleased to be here.

The dark-skinned woman who greets the INTERVIEWER is ELDRA. She is smartly dressed in a knee-length navy dress, with a matching tailored overcoat, and wears her hair in short tight, black curls. She looks far younger than her 70 years. The other two, who look much younger, are casually dressed. VEREEN is wearing jeans and CANDACE wears a long black skirt with a faded T-shirt. CANDACE has short dreadlocks and VEREEN has her pressed hair tied back. The younger women simultaneously look at the INTERVIEWER, moving their heads down as they observe her from head to toe. The INTERVIEWER pretends not to notice.

INTERVIEWER: What a wonderful venue and a good location.

ELDRA: The children do not mind coming down here because they know they will get something nice to eat.

VEREEN: Something nice to eat. You mean *you* come here to get something nice to eat. The kids don't eat the West Indian food. The only thing I have seen them rushing to get their hands on in here is that bubblegum machine on the counter.

CANDACE: The young people don't want West Indian food. They only want sweets.

VEREEN: And to my knowledge they do not serve chips here.

ELDRA: *(she ignores being corrected)* Thank goodness for that.

SCENE 3: The mentoring role – group interview with black women mentors

INTERVIEWER: Tell me about the project.

CANDACE: It provides supplementary classes in English and maths.

INTERVIEWER: Do you all teach these classes?

ELDRA: Very occasionally – I have been much too busy with my course.

CANDACE: We have all helped in the past when the tutors have been away.

VEREEN: Now with our studies we hardly have time for ourselves.

ELDRA: I mentor a 12-year-old girl, Tameka. She reminds me so much of myself when I was young *(laughs)*. I have to say, only in image mind. She is so lazy!

VEREEN: Still lazy!

ELDRA: Oh yes. The fact of the matter is these days young people have so many things to occupy their brains with. Coming to do some hard reading and writing is the last thing on their minds.

CANDACE: I mentor a 14-year-old girl. Every time we meet it's a real struggle. She is always late. There are times where she just does not show up at all. When she does attend, she is all dolled up with one side of her hair shaved off and those long painted nails of hers *(others laugh)*. She seems to spend the whole of our time together just looking at her nails while I talk at her. Her three favourite words to me are: 'Oh', 'Not really' and 'I suppose so!' *(everyone laughs)*. I never once heard her say 'Yes' or 'No' or even start a conversation. She likes to say 'Oh' to anything I tell her. I could say, 'Kadesha, you could be the Woman Scientist of the Year if you put your mind to it' and she would respond, 'Oh!' *(more laughing)*. And her mother looks just the same – the same nose ring and the same make-up. I cannot understand that style *(laughs)*.

INTERVIEWER: And who do you mentor, Vereen?

VEREEN: I mentor a young troublesome boy aged 10. When I first met him he was very sweet and after the four months, he was still very sweet. I could not understand how and why he needed a mentor because he looked like such a good boy. But of course, my impression of his sweetness did not last long. I am told he gets up to all sorts in the school, bullying other kids, shouting his mouth off.

INTERVIEWER: It seems like it has not been working out. Can you think of any reasons why?

The women are silent. All three look serious. After a few seconds a number of swift responses follow.

VEREEN: *(she shouts loudly)* Not working out! I have you know that the mentor project is a total success. We may have issues and will have our views about certain things but the relationships we have with our mentees are very positive relationships.

CANDACE: Oh yes, we are doing very well.

INTERVIEWER: I did not mean …

The INTERVIEWER is ignored.

ELDRA: Our sessions with our mentees are very productive.

VEREEN: Rashard may be unruly in school but he is never disrespectful of me.

CANDACE: The year is nearly up and they still come along. I meet with my mentee before the classes.

INTERVIEWER: What I meant was …

The INTERVIEWER is interrupted.

VEREEN: The scheme is serving a dual purpose. We encourage them. We are like second mothers to them. When the men were doing the mentoring, they would shout at the children, like drill sergeants.

CANDACE: We respect the children so they in turn respect us.

There is a lull and the INTERVIEWER speaks.

INTERVIEWER: You are all amazing and so incredible. I am so impressed with your success, while you are learning at the same time.

There is a moment's silence.

VEREEN: Well thank you very much. *(smiling)* You worried us for a minute.

CANDACE: It's good to know where black sisters are coming from.

The INTERVIEWER breathes a sign of relief. She feels reassured that all is not lost.

ELDRA: You should know that they are now getting a chance to show off their talents at the Town Hall. They are part of the Culture for Success Forum. My mentee is reciting a poem she wrote herself.

CANDACE: My Kadesha is part of the dancing troupe.

VEREEN: They are making my Rashard play the drums *(all laugh)*. Again!

INTERVIEWER: So what is the incentive …

CANDACE: *(interrupting, with a touch of anger)* What are you getting at?

VEREEN: We were chosen to be mentors because we were in education and there are large numbers of black girls at my college but they do not have the years of experience raising children and we feel proud that we were chosen.

CANDACE: Proud to have been chosen.

The words are repeated.

ELDRA: We like what we are doing and the community respects us for what we are doing.

CANDACE: *(obviously angry)* Are you thinking because we are mature women, you are surprised to hear about such positive relationships with younger people?

INTERVIEWER: No, not at all, on the contrary …

VEREEN: Education is important.

CANDACE: You must not question our motives for doing it. What do you mean incentives? We do not receive any payment for what we do. We are volunteers.

ELDRA: Money! We don't get money for this!

VEREEN: We need to put you right on that.

INTERVIEWER: I meant what are the incentives for the young people?

VEREEN: Oh, for the young people.

All the women are laughing. The INTERVIEWER takes another deep breath and waits for calmness to return.

CANDACE: We tell the young people that they must not waste their lives but we know that we may not be the best examples of role models as we are in education at our age but after so long we are still in their lives. The black male role models have given up on them.

VEREEN: Those young buppies …

CANDACE: Only wanted to place the experience on their CVs.

VEREEN: And then they were off like a shot!

Everyone laughs.

ELDRA: They were off after the first meeting!

VEREEN: After the first meeting!

ELDRA: Vanish!

VEREEN: No trace.

CANDACE: Absolutely no trace!

ELDRA: You have to have a heart …

VEREEN: … to mentor young people.

The three women speak fast, loudly, talking over each other and, at times, finishing each other's sentences.

CANDACE: Mentoring later at our age …

VEREEN: Means we are here to stay!

NARRATOR: The polyrhythmic realities have come into play. I reflected on black women who are learning and volunteering. Does lifelong learning in fact link to community engagement for older black women? Or is learning now a rather selfish act as the women pursue their separate and individual search for formal and further education? My response to the latter is no; this is not the case for the women in my study, as in this act where formal learning was being pursued the women were undertaking voluntary work of one form or another. In addition, they had a track record of working in the community.

INTERVIEWER: How did you find the mentoring project?

ELDRA: *(smiling)* It found us actually. They came looking for us at the college.

CANDACE: I think they found all of us the same way, through the colleges. But they found you, Eldra, from the Council.

NARRATOR: Up until that point the interview was a difficult one for me. The women were defensive and challenging. The return of polyrhythmic realities – albeit briefly – was a welcomed relief. I felt that the phrasing of my questions may have created anxiety in the women and I made a point of listening carefully to their responses. When Candace said 'It's good to know where black sisters are coming from', it made me think that the women may have prejudged me in some way. I felt they needed praise and reassurance for their efforts and when I did comment on my appreciation and respect for the work they were doing they seemed to be more comfortable and less angry.

SCENE 4: Formal learning – for whose benefit?

INTERVIEWER: Tell me about your college learning. What are you studying?

ELDRA: I want to start by telling you about my learning back home.

INTERVIEWER: Can we talk about learning in the UK first? Would you mind?

VEREEN: *(looks at ELDRA and speaks to her)* Candace and I do not have experiences of learning back home to share as we were very young when we came here – for, still a baby really, so it's best that you reflect on that later. We do not have that long for the interview anyway and you know how you like to go on.

CANDACE: Not that we don't want to hear but we will just be interfering because you know we would want to stop you.

ELDRA: It is a good thing I know you two. And please, do not put the interviewer off.

VEREEN: When Eldra talks about her experiences she is thorough so I hope you have enough space on your voice recorder! *(laughs)*

INTERVIEWER: So tell me about learning now?

ELDRA: I am at Hillviewdale Further Education College studying for an Explorers diploma. My course was recommended to me by my trade union and they are paying my course fees. The area I am studying concerns the levels of retirement pension received by retired West Indian people who go back home to the West Indies to retire. They all worked for the same long years in Britain but the level of pension they each receive is not the same. My tutor is a specialist in these sorts of areas and she has great knowledge of the public services and I am always marvelling at all the great educated people at my college and I do feel rather privileged and in awe of them all. As older students, we were told that we could research anything we wanted to and I had so many things that I wanted to explore but I chose my topic because I really could not understand why things were the way they were in respect to pension entitlements abroad because everyone deserves equal treatment and when you are old and poor in the West Indies, money is everything.

INTERVIEWER: What do you hope to gain from the course?

ELDRA: New knowledge, a sense of pride as well as a sense of achievement. I already have plenty of certificates for this and that course which I gained over the years but nothing of real substance so this diploma will be significant to me. I am learning so much and this course is finally going to give me some genuine academic qualifications. At first my project was going to be a study of black people in the trade union movement and fighting for justice in the workplace and I had started writing about Bill Morris and his rise to prominence in the trade union movement and I realized how much I already know about him. And what I really wanted to look at was something which I had very little knowledge about and I could then share that knowledge with other older West Indians and we might take collective action to do something about it.

INTERVIEWER: Wow, that's incredible and a really good reason for doing the course.

CANDACE: She is very good with words.

VEREEN: Politician!

INTERVIEWER: And so after the course, what will you do with your new learning – your college diploma?

ELDRA: First, I will breathe a sigh of relief and feel so happy that I have fulfilled a lifelong ambition and then I will be out there and everywhere advising union members and others! I will be a qualified voice for the people!

Everyone laughs.

SCENE 5: *Benefits of learning*

INTERVIEWER: And how do you think others would benefit from your learning?

ELDRA: The fact of the matter is my union will be benefiting greatly and by that I mean the organization and all its members. My union has a conference on working and planning for retirement, and I am going to lead a workshop there and discuss my project and I see it as a way of giving information to others and, for some, it will be a way of preparing for the future. The topic is really relevant to my trade union but I cannot reveal everything of course. Eldra continues: I am studying for a diploma because I want to tackle social injustice! But on the Explorers programme, I am finally spreading my wings and doing something for myself.

VEREEN: We can honestly say that being on a college access course allows us an opportunity for independence and freedom when we can finally spread our wings!

NARRATOR: This phrase seems to have a real significance for the women.

INTERVIEWER: What does lifelong learning mean to you, Candace?

CANDACE: A chance to learn at my convenience. A few years back, there was stigma attached to studying for a degree beyond the age of 40. It was usually just older African men who would study at that late age, with their suit and briefcase. We used to just laugh and see this as very embarrassing but not anymore. We actually respect them now.

INTERVIEWER: What are you learning and why?

CANDACE: I am learning on the access course because I want to raise self-esteem in the community. There really is not a lot of that in the community and it's as if everyone has lost all hope.

NARRATOR: Both Eldra and Candace have talked about their learning as a way of giving something back before they have said much about what they are gaining in terms of their own development. This seems to highlight how strongly they feel about their caring responsibilities for others and younger generations.

CANDACE: There were a lot of expectations placed on us as young women or young girls and even as young children coming from the Caribbean at the time we came. It was like we had all these opportunities and why have we not got ourselves a string of qualifications because education was free. We may not have a Caribbean accent. Some would say our accent was not a barrier but, in our household, it was just about a work ethic and that was all that we saw. Our parents worked long hours. There was no parent, no aunt, no uncle in education. Everyone was working in factories, on the buses, on the trains. Our mother was working night and day at any old job and so while we wanted to do better educationally, we were not capable of doing that much better. But our parents expected so much and other family members expected so much because we came here so young but when my brothers came along, I was the one looking after all of them when my mum and dad both went out to work. It was like my younger brothers were my own children; I had to bathe them, feed them and then clean the house, wash the clothes and cook everyone's dinner. It was like I had a full-time job too! How on earth could I have done better in school? I had lost my education.

INTERVIEWER: Indeed.

SCENE 6: Lost education in a British Caribbean colony: Formal learning for whose benefit?

CANDACE: And you know what? When I got 'Unclassified' in CSE Maths at school, my father called me lazy!

Everyone laughs.

VEREEN: I did not know that classification existed!

ELDRA: But how can anyone fail such a basic assessment?

Everyone laughs.

NARRATOR: What Candace describes about her lost education and all the expectations being focused on work reminds me of reflections in other research. African Caribbean women, according to Carby, 'were encouraged and chose to come to Britain precisely to work. Ideologically they were seen as "naturally" suitable for the lowest paid, most menial jobs' (Carby, 1997: 48).

INTERVIEWER: You are describing a form of oppression and perhaps …

CANDACE: *(interrupting)* I knew of girls who came to the UK at the same age as I did. Had I not had so much responsibility, who knows, I may have got the good A level grades to be able to go. I just about got a Grade 2 CSE in English.

ELDRA: Those early education school days were so important.

VEREEN: And I think we forget what racism felt like in those days. There was a boy in my primary school who would keep on spitting at me for no reason.

ELDRA: For no reason?

VEREEN: He used to call me wog.

ELDRA: Well, you know the reason.

VEREEN: Yes but at the time I just felt it was for no reason whatsoever – because I never did him anything.

CANDACE: Well that's where you went wrong. Do you think anyone at my school could get away with doing that to me?

VEREEN: You see that was the difference – all the Jamaican kids were tough and stood up for themselves but we were timid.

ELDRA: You see the small island people had a different mentality altogether.

VEREEN: You are talking about us as if we are from a different planet.

CANDACE: How could we have ever got far with our education when we had to cope with racist abuse at that age? So many black children would ignore it and just take the abuse, the intimidation and the violation.

VEREEN: We had a bad start at home and a bad time in the schools and this is why I want to get my teachers' training qualification to do something serious out there.

CANDACE: Good self-esteem is so important and we were never ever given that at home, in the schools, nowhere.

ELDRA: You cannot blame your mother or your father because the only jobs some of them could get were the night jobs.

NARRATOR: I recognized that the women were linking their own experiences of parents absent from educational involvement and with limited expectations about their achievements to ways they could now, as adults, change things for future generations through their own influence in education.

CANDACE: Yes, and that is why and how our early education suffered. There was not anyone there to help us with our homework and no one to praise us when we were doing well. How could we have done any better? My dad always goes on about spending all his money on buying us children a whole volume of *Encyclopaedia Britannia* [sic] and we turn out to be damn fools.

VEREEN: Did he really say that?

CANDACE: He'd say it all the time.

VEREEN: That is so awful.

CANDACE: And did you know that in one of those encyclopaedias it said that the shape of the black man's brain is far inferior to the white man's brain and that we could never ever be as intelligent as the white man? Yes, those were the books my father wanted me to read from.

VEREEN: No wonder you all rebelled.

CANDACE: There was always war in our house over education. I lost interest and could not be bothered with it for a while.

INTERVIEWER: What was the curriculum like when you were at school and how do you think it helped you?

VEREEN: I really enjoyed school when I got to be a teenager. It was the best part of my life for a while. We did domestic science, art, classical studies, English literature and the British constitution. I really enjoyed it all.

VEREEN: We learnt about Homer, Odysseus and Oedipus. I really enjoyed school. I did not want to leave.

CANDACE: *(peering at Vereen disapprovingly)* I left as soon as I got the chance. They kicked me out for regularly not wearing the uniform.

VEREEN: I stayed on but failed my A levels.

CANDACE: But you know even if we had got the grades, nobody talked about university. You had to go straight out to work to bring some money into the house. University was not an option. I remember only one black girl from our year going to university in the end.

VEREEN: That famous one you always talk about. But her family was not from the Caribbean – and her father was a diplomat.

CANDACE: This is very true.

SCENE 7: *Reflecting on lifelong learning*

INTERVIEWER: And what does lifelong learning mean to you now, Vereen?

VEREEN: Lifelong learning is a window of opportunity which we would be a fool not to pass through. After all we have waited so long and the chance comes along at this time. Being on benefits means I don't have to pay for everything because there is no way that I would be able to afford it otherwise.

INTERVIEWER: Vereen, tell me some more about what you are learning and why?

VEREEN: I am learning in order to gain a teacher's training diploma so that I can help empower others.

INTERVIEWER: Anything to add, Eldra?

ELDRA: Back home, we did not have qualification but if you could read and write you were up another level – well above the ordinary people on the island. As a matter of fact, education and status is highly admired in the West Indies.

VEREEN: Everywhere, I think you will find Eldra.

CANDACE: Status is a big thing in the Caribbean.

VEREEN: When I go back to Grenada on holiday, my father does not allow my mother to speak with the workers in the yard and we were not allowed to play together or eat together with the people who worked in our gardens.

ELDRA: Some of us were considered the education elite in our village but we did not have a paper qualification between us! *(laughs)*

VEREEN: Class is such a big issue in the Caribbean.

ELDRA: My father died when we were very young and there was a time straight after school when my older sister and I had to go to the farm to collect the yams and my sister would carry a sack of yams on her head while I walked behind her. She would always know when the high school boys from the college would be coming round the bend. Like lightning the sack of yams would be off her head and in the ditch. She would then compose herself and stroll along the road. As soon as the boys were out of sight she would pull onto my hands and beckon me over to pick up the yams from the ditch.

CANDACE: *(sighs)* That story was for your benefit. We have heard it several times.

ELDRA ignores the comment.

VEREEN: Eldra, you will have plenty of time to talk about 'back home' later.

CANDACE: But you know we talk about class, but the significance of a good education and educational values and aspirations was always instilled in us from an early age.

VEREEN: We know the value of education.

CANDACE: My mother told me when she was a young adult in the West Indies, the island did not have a prime minister but a governor-general. It was not until she came to England that she heard there was a prime minister for her country of birth. The governor-general was very interested in education for the children and she always said that he was a good man. Because there was no radio in the house, she did not get to see any newspapers, and television did not exist back in her day, but she remembers hearing the governor-general speak on RadioVision in the town and he was saying that education was our saviour and we must all learn to read and write for a better future. Every month when my mother went to the market to sell the ground provisions, she would stand by the RadioVision tree with all the other country people and listen to the governor-general speaking the Queen's English. My mother always said, 'Education is our saviour.' That man had a big influence on her.

INTERVIEWER: Thank you very much for all your valuable insights and for your time.

CANDACE: Vereen and I both have to leave now.

As VEREEN and CANDACE open the door to depart, there is a familiar aroma of fried plantain fritters and the shouts of women still giving orders from the shop front.

CANDACE: *(looking back at the INTERVIEWER)* Let me get you a drink and a patty. Are you vegetarian? *(smiles)*

ACT 8: Sisters representing: A story of learning for political activism

CAST OF CHARACTERS

NARRATOR	The INTERVIEWER speaks to the audience, as an aside
INTERVIEWER	Speaks directly to the characters
LIZ	Aged 53, from Dominica
JOYCE	Aged 69, from Guyana
CAROLE	Aged 60, from Jamaica
JULIA	Aged 61, from Dominica

SCENE 1: *Introduction*

The INTERVIEWER enters the green refurbished open-plan annexe and goes to sit at the furthest end of the expansive cafeteria. It is early afternoon at the main campus of the university. She observes students, with shoulder bags, headphones and mobile phones talking loudly as they hurry to pick up trays and queue up for their snacks. Then she sees a small group of older black women laden with books and folders in both hands. One woman from the group stops and tries to wave to acknowledge the INTERVIEWER as they move carefully past a hive of chattering students. The women who are about to meet the INTERVIEWER are elected members of two local authorities and are undertaking a part-time Diploma in Higher Education.

SCENE 2: *Sisters outside the council chamber*

After introductions and signing of consent forms and other formalities, the INTERVIEWER addresses the group.

INTERVIEWER: So you are representing different political parties but you are learning together?

JULIA: Joyce and I are from different parties but we are on the same council.

JOYCE: Yes, we are from different political parties and at one stage we did not talk to each other. When some of us did, it was across the council chamber and it used to be quite acrimonious! But here at the college we support each other.

Mild laughter.

JULIA: I don't really think we support each other somehow. Yes to a point but not entirely.

LIZ: In the classroom we support each other's points of view.

CAROLE: Because we have to think together.

JOYCE: Not always. In fact you always argue against everything I say.

CAROLE: The course has brought us together!

LIZ: We are even helping each other with our studies when we are here. You cannot deny that.

The other women appear to openly consider the statement.

INTERVIEWER: So tell me about your learning prior to the course.

LIZ: I myself did have good, happy experiences in the schools system – but the black brothers our age suffered worse. In the early seventies when my partner was aged 16, 17, he was being picked up and thrown into prison cells left, right and centre for doing nothing.

JOYCE: The same for my husband. Just being in the wrong place at the wrong time – and you know it is only recently that he has revealed this to me. We have been together for 27 years and this has just come out. Never come out before, only just recently.

CAROLE: That kind of thing marks you for life.

NARRATOR: The women did not respond to my specific question and chose to divulge other matters. It was at this stage that I considered the story-like qualities to my data and recalled Earthy and Cronin's (2008) observation that as narrative researchers we do not always set out to collect narratives as stories but instead discover the presence of story-like qualities in an interviewee's account during our later analysis of a study. I also reflected that by openly sharing their experiences the women were learning about similarities in their own experiences.

The women return to the question.

JULIA: Although I had a good education in North London I still did not do as well as my parents would have liked me to do.

JOYCE: My mother thought I did remarkably well with gaining O levels and she thought I would be a doctor with that.

Everyone laughs.

JOYCE: I used to work, work and work. One year I had three jobs going all at once – night cleaning, day cleaning, filling up cocktail stick bottles in the afternoons – oh and hairdressing in my back room!

Everyone laughs.

JOYCE: I was too tired to even think of studying after that. You cannot learn when you are always tired. For a long time I put off education. I would start a college course at the local college but could never finish it. Things just got in the way.

LIZ: Like your rebel days working with the short-life housing group.

NARRATOR: The women have clearly already learnt a lot about each other.

JOYCE: Yes and things like that. But the children mainly kept me busy. Education was a luxury. Something you would do if you had time on your hands.

JULIA: When I first got into politics, I was up and down so much, knocking on people's doors, attending meetings till midnight sometimes, preparing the sandwiches and making the teas, clearing up – my name only got put forward at the last minute. They thought it was a long shot – I would never win – but I did!

All the women laugh.

LIZ: And the party has never been the same since!

More laughter.

JOYCE: I, on the other hand, had all what it takes – looks, charm, a certificated education, excellent employment record, but after 15 years working hard in the constituency party they have only just taken me on board and recognize what I have to offer!

There is raucous laughter and words such as 'Only just now' are being repeated.

JOYCE: When I got accepted to the panel I got selected at my first interview. The ward members had no hesitation in voting for me.

LIZ: Really?

CAROLE: *(returning to an earlier assertion)* But what education were you talking about, Joyce? You mean that little City and Guilds from that bad reputation college?

Others laugh.

JOYCE: And with my two O levels – it is still an education. And what do you have to speak of my dear?

Everyone laughs. The women exchange notes and banter with each other for a while.

JULIA: Remember when we are here, we are speaking confidentially. We are not going to disclose our business elsewhere.

There is a moment of silence and the women appear serious in contemplation as if uncomfortable with the last statement.

NARRATOR: As the women got together outside their formal meeting places, in informal gatherings, I could observe the polyrhythmic realities as they shared their experiences, shedding light on other areas of their lives. Despite their political differences, they appeared to have a great deal in common.

JULIA: In politics we get an education because there is so much learning that goes on minute-by-minute.

INTERVIEWER: What type of learning?

JULIA: Learning to get on with others of different perspectives.

JOYCE: Learning to cope when you are being insulted.

LIZ: You are thrown in at the deep end in politics.

JULIA: Swim or sink.

CAROLE: You are not always chosen for your talent or what you can do but if you happen to be in the right place at the right time!

JOYCE: And if your face fits.

JULIA: I disagree

Laughter. The women keep repeating 'if your politics fits' and 'if your face fits'.

JOYCE: You don't even have to speak good English to be a councillor in Foresdale Town.

All the women laugh.

LIZ: You are just a name on the ballot paper. If your party is strong in that ward then you are a certainty.

JOYCE: Not always the case. In my ward people knew me very well.

The women ignore JOYCE's statement.

JULIA: But when you get in – my word you have to be tough. Stand your ground! Be smart!

JOYCE: Otherwise the humiliation you receive can kill you!

There is embarrassed laughter.

JOYCE: Weak women don't last long in politics. You cannot be bashful and you cannot use your grandchildren as an excuse to get out of meetings because you are not supposed to be minding them! That's what our children are there for – to look after their own children. You have to conform to the British way of doing things. You get chastised by everybody if you do not show up for a meeting with a lame excuse like childcare. Not at our age anyway! *(laughs)* And when you are black you get double the pressure.

INTERVIEWER: Tell me about that.

JOYCE: It is quite a responsibility. You don't want to let down the side. Black people around you are looking at you all the time – especially your immediate family. You want to do the right thing but you have to think of so many different things – the local papers for one thing. They are so quick to want to get a quote from you. You cannot continue with your previous way of life in the same way. Before I came on the council I still had some time for church. But now I have so much to do on the council.

LIZ: When you go to church it is just more casework building up anyway.

CAROLE: If colonialism had not brought us Christianity, church would not be such a priority for us.

This statement is provocative.

JOYCE: Don't be blasphemous. Where would we be without the church?

CAROLE: What's wrong with praying to the almighty at home!

JULIA: Well as black women, church or no church, I agree, we feel the pressure more. We always have to play catch-up because we think about our shortcomings more and try to do the right thing. When we are feeling real pressure on the council, we cannot say we don't understand or that we have a hard job getting to understand some of the complex documents.

LIZ: We just spend our time trying to get through it all, reading late at night. We are just trying to make proper sense of the issues. We cannot bluff our way through things because I don't think we feel we have the vocabulary to be able to do that. We need to read more.

CAROLE: But you know how it is, we don't like getting help because the opposition will be quick to say we are not up to the job.

JULIA: Here at the university for two hours every two weeks, we have freedom to learn. We can relax. We can make mistakes and know we can ask for help from the lecturer.

JOYCE: But you know on the council, we know so many other members who we suspect might not be up to the job. At every meeting we are seeing how other elected members stumble and fall. Oh yes, they have their moments. For example, Morash is always getting it wrong.

JULIA: But he is a man and he gets away with it.

LIZ: Ruthlessness is being assertive.

JULIA: They listen to him.

CAROLE: We make a lot of notes at these meeting. To try to keep up.

JOYCE: But these notes make no sense to us if the truth be known.

Everyone laughs.

JULIA: When I look at my notes I think ... What kind of crazy writing is this?

CAROLE: What is that! What did I write there? *(turns to the INTERVIEWER)* No joke.

JOYCE: When we think back, over the years it has not been easy for us.

CAROLE: It is a real steep learning curve.

JULIA: But we have to represent.

LIZ: I think this is the fastest learning curve for many of us older black women.

INTERVIEWER: What do you mean? Why?

CAROLE: Because, mostly we have just hit the ground running – everyone wants you to deal with their complaints as a priority. Everyone tells you they have an urgent case; you have to learn how to use a mobile phone properly, send fast emails, make proper telephone calls to senior staff at the council – regular!

JULIA: Girl, I have never been so frightened in all my life!

LIZ: Getting it wrong. Making big mistakes … Getting blamed …

CAROLE: When you representing people you have to get it right. But it is pressure. It is pure pressure. That type of pressure I did not feel when I was running the black women's Fight Back project.

JULIA: *(speakingly jokingly and looking at JOYCE)* A good education would have made a difference, we know that. How many times do we take 10 years writing a simple message in a little email? And some of us are college educated.

Everyone laughs.

JOYCE: You think I am taking chances with that sort of thing? When you push that button – you can't take it back you know. Remember that.

INTERVIEWER: *(looking at JULIA)* What do you mean when you say 'a good education would have made a difference'?

JULIA: Well you have to have confidence when you write quickly. If your grammar slips it is very frustrating. You don't want officers taking advantage of you because they see you as a damn fool.

Mild laughter.

LIZ: But they know how it is. I am sure other members write foolishness at times. You see the thing is some things we take too seriously. We waste time thinking about nonsense – the small things. We are our worst enemies.

NARRATOR: I was mindful at this stage that I now needed to focus the interview on the nature of formal learning.

Image and text courtesy of Syl Noelle

Figure 4: Dou Dou, Syl and Bol – 'We older sisters – just contemplating the learning commess in the church hall'

SCENE 3: Learning and professional development

INTERVIEWER: And what about the higher education Diploma in Local Government?

JULIA: This diploma could provide me with a pathway to a degree. It is a diploma, which I know I will be proud of. After all it comes from a university!

INTERVIEWER: What can you tell me about the course?

LIZ: It deals with the current state of local government by looking at the past and considering the future.

INTERVIEWER: It sounds very interesting.

JULIA: We have local government experts coming to talk to us.

CAROLE: We have to write essays about problems we face in our role – we can pick up any area – working with tenants, communicating messages to council and the area we represent. There is a professional development aspect looking at relating to very senior officers and dealing with new legislation and its impact on services.

JOYCE: We are attending university two hours every two weeks for three terms and we are getting so much from it!

The women go on to eagerly discuss the commitment to their studies and the pressure of political life.

Review of Act 8

It was clear from this act that black sisterhood was a most significant factor for the women participants. Despite experiencing hostile local political environments at times, they came together to pursue their passion for formal learning in their later years. Such learning could help them overcome a number of challenges in their personal and political lives.

Chapter 7

Reflections on the (mis)education of the black sister

ACT 9: Eldra's story

CAST OF CHARACTERS

NARRATOR	The INTERVIEWER speaks to the audience, as an aside
INTERVIEWER	Speaks directly to the characters
ELDRA	Aged 70, from St Vincent; came to the UK in 1959, aged 20

SCENE 1: *A full life caring for the community*

NARRATOR: Two women members of the Black Learners and Achievers Project left the room and I proceeded to conduct a one-to-one interview with Eldra, who was born in St Vincent but grew up in St Lucia and came to the UK in 1959 at the age of 20. Unlike many of her peers, she did not marry or have children, which she said 'was a blessing in disguise' as she would have had the 'perfect excuse' for not achieving her educational goals. She is a governor at a primary school in Lincolnvale, a community mentor to a young person and, up until very recently, was also a local councillor, having served on the city council for almost 25 years. As a result of her time on the council, she holds membership of four local boards concerned with community health, education, social housing and civic relations. Such membership allows her frequent access to meeting rooms at the town hall. Eldra told me she is very well known and respected in the Lincolnvale community and claims she had a good working relationship with the council officers, many of whom, she says, believe she is still a serving city councillor.

SCENE 2: *Educating Mistress Eldra*

INTERVIEWER: So what does lifelong learning mean to you?

ELDRA: Lifelong learning means everything to me as without it I would not have been able to catch up on my education and today I am finally closer to getting my hands on that piece of paper that tells the world that I have a college education and a diploma to prove it. I am 70 years of age and have no educational qualifications to speak of but as a child I was considered to have a very bright future, and other children and the older people in my parish had high hopes for me. Not long after I came to England, I heard that people back home were asking questions about me like: 'Where is Eldra?'; 'What is she doing?'; 'She must be a scientist by now or maybe a lawyer!' *(chuckles)*

INTERVIEWER: How did you cope with such expectations?

ELDRA: I had to put up with it all and had to lay low and keep myself to myself for a good long while *(laughs out loud)*. I did not venture back to St Lucia until a good many years [later]. The folks expected so much of me and before I became a councillor in Lincolnvale people often used to say how much I looked like a school mistress and I found that highly amusing because, growing up, my grandmother used to call me 'Mistress Eldra' – that was her nickname for me as she thought I was a bright child. She was my guiding light, my guardian angel and my first and most influential primary teacher, who taught me so much about life and, most importantly, that good education and good appearance went hand-in-hand.

NARRATOR: Eldra responded to my questions in detail and in a clear, assertive manner. I could not discern a specific Caribbean accent but she frequently used Caribbean colloquialisms when referring to events that had occurred 'back home'. However, she pronounced her words carefully, and her manner and style gave me the impression that she was well educated. However, during the interview Eldra revealed that she had no formal educational qualifications and had left school at the age of 13 to care for her sick grandmother, the former village postmistress.

SCENE 3: Books are more important than walking hammocks

INTERVIEWER: Tell me more about your early learning and the influence of your grandmother.

ELDRA: If I am honest, I can tell you now that most of my early learning came from my grandmother who raised me from an early age, and both her and my mother went to the convent school and all who attended convent school were considered the best educated. Of course you had to be one of the well-off and privileged girls on the island to get a place inside that place. My grandmother cared about my education and I know she also cared about the education of the poor children in the village.

NARRATOR: 'She also cared about the education of the poor' reminded me of Collins's (2000a) reference to black women caring for the wider community.

ELDRA: She and I – we would sit together for hours on the front veranda as she read history to me and, on occasions, while she was reading, she would pause and we would observe people in the hills in the distance, walking slowly from a neighbouring village, carrying the sick to the hospital in shining white walking hammocks that glowed in the morning sunshine.

INTERVIEWER: Walking hammocks?

ELDRA: You should know that I have given that name to what I witnessed back then. Actually the real name for this display was commonly known as 'Wavet Garçons' or 'cockroach boys' – that's what the old folks called the procession which was a regular feature of village life back home in the 1930s and early 1940s and it was quite a ritual, only performed by drop-out school boys from poorer families. These walking hammocks were made with a large white sheet, provided by the church, which was tied tightly at each end on to long bamboo poles. The sick person was carried for miles to hospital by two and sometimes four boys, depending on how heavy the invalid person was.

INTERVIEWER: The boys would carry out such an important task?

ELDRA: *(looking serious)* These were strong boys who would walk in the hot sun and take it in turns to carry the hammock and they would only stop when one of them got tired. Back home in those days the community supported each other as much as possible because, for most people, there was no money for transport, and as payment for their arduous journeys the boys received one dumpling each and a little piece of salt fish to share between them. The schoolboys who performed these tasks were never, ever the brightest in the school and their families could not afford books to help them learn and they were usually looked-after by the church. My grandmother gave money to the church and if ever she spotted the walking hammocks on a school morning she would shake her head in disgust. Before I started school I used to hear her mutter under her breath words like: 'Holy Trinity should be ashamed. Instead of giving the children books to learn and gain self-respect, they are providing them with tools for walking the dead. What damnation!' She would then hold on to me tightly and tell me how relieved she was that we were not living in poverty and that I must make sure I was in school every day so I could get a good education then I would never ever be poor like the 'Wavet Garçons'.

NARRATOR: I reflected on the significance of books. It was clear that Eldra's grandmother had instilled in her the idea that books were a vital part of learning.

INTERVIEWER: So books were very important to your grandmother?

ELDRA: As a matter of fact, not just my grandmother but to everyone back then. When I was growing up, in the British West Indies, you had to have books to learn and the same books were all over the islands and we thought they were only in St Lucia at the time, but as we grew into adults we found out that every island in the colonies had the same books. We had to go to Delancey's in the Boulevard to buy our school books and I knew that everyone in our school had a school book, unless you were very poor but most poor families still found a way to get their children the books because learning was important and the teachers expected everyone to have a school book.

INTERVIEWER: What type of books did you learn from?

ELDRA: The school books then were called *The Royal Crown Readers* and the contents gave us invaluable insights into the British Empire, the great men and women of England, like Queen Victoria and Lord Nelson. Written on the back of each of our books were the words 'British Possession', and as children we found out that in other islands there was a Dutch Possession as well as a French Possession edition. We in St Lucia had the British Possession and we were very proud of that fact because it was considered the best by all who possessed one. Each book cost one penny but if Mr Delancey, the shop owner, knew your family well then each year you would get the books for free but he only gave one copy of a reader to one family, so most children in the same household shared the readers and passed them on to a younger child. We had no other books to learn from apart from an exercise book with the times table which we had to learn by heart.

NARRATOR: I considered Eldra's pride when speaking about her school books and how they gave her insights into the British Empire and key figures in British history. I then wondered about the nature of books available to Caribbean children like her at that particular time and found myself remembering bell hooks's rather different assessment: 'No history books used in public schools informed us about racial imperialism, as instead, we were given romantic notions of the "new world"' (hooks, 1994: 373). For Eldra, who grew up in a British colonized island, it appeared that as long as the books were issued by the British education system, the contents would be invaluable.

ACT 10: Reading with the Caribbean matriarch

SCENE 1: Crown Standard Readers

INTERVIEWER: When did your grandmother start reading to you?

ELDRA takes a few moments to reflect.

ELDRA: My grandmother first started reading to me in 1943 when I was 4 years old. That was the time that my mother went to live in the town with my grandmother's sister, as she was recommended for a job in the public records office. My grandmother raised my sister and me until my older sister was old enough to go to the convent school and then moved to live with my mother in town. At one point when we were growing up, my older sister had all the school books and at first I did not have any of my own as I had trouble with her over the sharing of the books. She was not really into education in the way that I was and she never really took learning seriously, I don't think. But yet still she did not want to share her books with me and if it had not been for my grandmother getting involved and reading to me, I would not have had sight of any of the *Crown Standard Readers* that we were meant to be sharing. Delancey only gave one first and one second *Crown Reader* to one family and my sister kept the books like they were her own. But my grandmother saw to it that she shared and when she went off to the convent I had access to both readers.

INTERVIEWER: Your grandmother read to you only from these readers?

ELDRA: My grandmother always read to me from the standard issue *Crown Reader* in such a flamboyant fashion as if she was performing on the stage. She had amazing diction and such dramatic hand gestures. She would read to me from my sister's first and second *Standard Crown Readers* and her beautiful voice was strong and her words would echo loudly as she read to me about the gallant efforts of Sir Francis Drake, Sir Walter Raleigh, Horatio Nelson and the battle of Trafalgar. She read in such poetic style that each time she looked like resting I would flick through the pages quickly to find interesting images of other great men, and kings and queens, ships and battles depicting the history of the Great British Empire. She would share with me all the glories of the Empire and, as she read, my grandmother's voice level would rise up high and then low and then rise up again and I thought she had all the time in the world and that she would be reading to me forever.

SCENE 2: *Tempestuous tales*

INTERVIEWER: You seem to remember those days so very well?

ELDRA: *(smiles)* You see, the thing was, as a child I was so excited by her performances that when I became proficient enough to be able to read to her myself, I would use similar hand gestures and stress my words in the same manner in which she had done. But there came a time when I was a lot older, about aged 7 maybe, when my grandmother showed the first signs of having an illness. At that time, she clearly was in a great deal of pain because she suddenly slowed down and started reading in a slow monotone manner and there she had no hand gestures and she took longer to finish her sentences. I recalled a storm outside, and the part of the book that she was reading from concerned battles across deep tempestuous waters, and I imagined the sounds of clashing ships. The readings had become truly vivid and exciting and I did not want my grandmother to stop as Lord Horatio Nelson, I believed, had lost an eye or an arm and he was about to make a decisive decision.

NARRATOR: Reading about British history was an important part of the British education system but the history of the colonized was never part of the curriculum for first-generation African Caribbean women.

ELDRA: I was mesmerized by what I was hearing and I just wanted my grandmother to finish reading, and although I was aware she was making signs for me to fetch her some water, I totally ignored her requests and shouted: 'Finish reading that part!' I was fearful of going outside to the yard to battle my way through the rain to the pipe, fearing obeah and what I could see looked like a hurricane outside.

INTERVIEWER: You have some vivid recollections?

ELDRA: I blocked out precisely what my grandmother had said in response to my outburst but recall what my older sister had told me about what she was told was my grandmother's sharp response to me that day: 'Salop, salop, little salop! Mistress Eldra, you had better go fetch water and bring your little black [!] self right here to read until you drop!' From that day on, the soothing side to my grandmother's amazing voice was no more.

That day I saw the first sign of her illness and I took over the reading of the *Crown Readers*.

INTERVIEWER: How did you find that reading role?

ELDRA: Now you know something? I did take over the reading and my grandmother come back stronger and about two years later my mother eventually sent for my older sister because she managed to get her a place at the convent school in town. I was not old enough to go there and so I stayed with my grandmother and continued my learning at the local village school until my grandmother's health deteriorated.

SCENE 3: Education, assimilation and community

INTERVIEWER: Did you try to get into education when you first arrived in the UK?

ELDRA: I have to declare that when I came to England I just stayed in the house just caring for my godmother and then my godfather and I didn't dare ask about university as that would seem so ungrateful, as there was illness to consider and I had a home and was being well looked after myself. I didn't even think about my appearance because I had so much to do in the house and I had lost all my enthusiasm for education at that time. It was as if I was so disappointed with coming to England, the Great Empire that I had learnt so much about, and here it was a dull, lonely, depressing place. I was in a big house with no friends apart from my godparents, who came from St Vincent, but after they passed things really changed and I started mixing with people my own age and got stuck into working in the community and I have never looked back since.

INTERVIEWER: And today?

ELDRA: It is so different – it is like I was 15 again, free again, but this time I am in education and focused just on myself for a change.

INTERVIEWER: Today, in what ways are you able to help others in the community with the things you are learning?

ELDRA: I am not certain but, to be quite blunt, even though I am no longer a councillor the community members still come to my door seeking my help and I am still available to do my best for them. I get on very well with the council officers and can call on them at any time. But not now, I am giving them a break because I am at college and studying hard!

SCENE 4: *Impact of early alternative learning*

INTERVIEWER: Tell me about any regrets you have about your early learning.

ELDRA: On so many occasions I know I was bound to be spelling some words incorrectly but the family and the community trusted me because they knew that I had been raised by the postmistress (my grandmother) and that I was considered a smart, mature child *(laughs)*. I received a great deal of praise for my letter-writing and at the time I never really felt that I was spelling most people's names blatantly incorrectly. I thought that I was being careful about getting it right and I have to admit that I enjoyed the praise and the status I received for helping out. But I do regret not getting the pronunciation of names right.

INTERVIEWER: How has this impacted on your learning today?

ELDRA: As a child I looked at words on paper but I was intrigued with the pronunciation of words and so was very hung up about listening and spelling things correctly. Today getting people's names wrong is something that I am nervous about.

INTERVIEWER: Was that because of the experience with your headmaster?

ELDRA: Not just that. There was a fairly recent incident, or catastrophe as I like to call it, when I attended our family reunion and I received a rather rude awakening.

ELDRA remains silent for a few moments. She looks upwards solemnly.

INTERVIEWER: What was the catastrophe?

ELDRA: *(sighs)* I was actually quite shaken up when a senior, very well-educated male member of the family confronted me in public and I have to admit that I felt humiliated. It all came about when here in the UK we were preparing for our family reunion and my niece asked me for some help with putting the names of the family members (on my mother's side) up on the chart and I was a great help to my niece as I could clearly remember the names of a large number of our St Lucian family members as a result of writing all those family letters. But, of course, the names of the family members were never ever spelt out to me and even if they were, when they were spelt, they did not always sound right to me and so I would spell the names in the way that I thought they ought to have been spelt. Where I was told Theresa, I would spell 'Teresa' – in the same way it was pronounced to me. When I heard Beula, I spelt it 'Bula'. It was pointless asking my aunts or uncles as, in my view, they would often make a very poor attempt at spelling out the names and there were times when I would deliberately put a flowery spin on a family member's name. And strange as it may sound, some have been known to reply back, using my exact same adapted spelling! In such circumstances, Eugene became 'Ugene' and Eugenie became 'Ugeanie' and 'Tado' should have been Theodore, and so when my aunt pronounced Dudley to me I embarrassingly wrote it as 'Dodlay'.

INTERVIEWER: How did you know the names were not spelt correctly?

ELDRA: It came to a head for me on that fatal day, when the family patriarch, Uncle Dudley, arrived at the family reunion – all the way from the USA, having been the first relative to have left St Lucia as a young man, and not only did he arrive to celebrate the family reunion, it was also his 80th birthday. He was like a professor in the family, very well respected and a very well-travelled man who despite coming from the States and never having set a foot in England, spoke with a strong British accent. *(shouts)* 'Who is the fool that has put this nonsense family tree together?' I remember him asking *loudly and rudely.*

It was in the millennium year and, at the age of 61, I had all the confidence knocked out of me in one fell swoop! So many family members found out that day that, after all these years, I was not as clever as they had thought. I had come to the family reunion in St Lucia, in my smart Chanel suit, all the way from Great Britain of all places, to hear my Uncle Dudley speaking in the Queen's English and going through a long list of names that I had not spelt correctly! On that day, I detected no family member of mine making any attempt to conceal their obnoxious laughing!

Review of Act 10

Eldra's responses to my questions were clear and detailed. Presented almost like an oral history (Gilbert, 2008: 430) account, she provided illuminating insights into the education system in the colonized British Caribbean islands at a particular time in their history. Her accounts of her personal lifelong learning journeys were traumatic and eventful and her journey still continues, as she nears her ultimate goals.

The stories in this book clearly show that older black women bring their own lived experiences, distinct ways of working together and a desire for learning that combine in a unique and valuable contribution to improving their local communities (Antrobus, 2004) and to the learning for future generations. It is clear that older black women learners can free themselves of past learning barriers to influence and learn in partnership with others. They are able to establish their own learning spaces within self-constructed communities of practice, where their shared ethnic and cultural heritage enables them to excel together as learners and influence their own and others' emancipation.

So far this book has revealed a previously unheard voice in lifelong learning. It is a voice that is becoming highly significant as mixed communities grow and vulnerable older people could well become isolated as local welfare resources and facilities are cut. This voice must be heard. It expresses the desire for learning for emancipation and wellbeing in an unexplored and neglected area. The work of Withnall (2000), Jackson (2005) and Jamieson (2007) into lifelong learning and older learners is here extended to include a black feminist perspective. In the on-going debate around ageing and learning, these narratives seek to highlight the central role of the older black woman learner as a key figure in promoting informal learning in gendered settings where distinct conversational strategies and polyrhythmic realities are employed in an effort to tackle deficits in learning as well as loneliness and isolation in ageing urban societies.

ACT 11: Reflecting on a British colonial education

SCENE 1: Pronunciation, holding back and shame

INTERVIEWER: What happened then?

ELDRA: After my sister left, my grandmother and I got on really well and she went on to correct me when I pronounced my words incorrectly and ever since her strict tutoring I have always fixated on getting pronunciation right.

NARRATOR: It was clear that Eldra thought that as she was being read to by her knowledgeable grandmother, her learning had been of a good standard – perhaps better than that of her peers.

INTERVIEWER: How useful was it? Being able to pronounce words correctly I mean?

ELDRA: Well it was useful up to a point and I am still learning, and had I stayed in school it may have been exceedingly useful in my adult life.

INTERVIEWER: What do you mean by 'up to a point'?

ELDRA: You see the thing was, as I grew up, older members of my extended family would come to me to write their letters to other family members living overseas in places like Guadeloupe, Martinique, Curaçao, Puerto Rico and St Croix. I enjoyed that role – of writing letters – and considered myself a very well-respected young lady in the community at that time. After all, I was the one who was entrusted to write all their personal letters, and had insights into their private lives. Although you need to know that I later went on to believe that this role in the community had a profound influence on the poor progress I made in achieving my educational goals.

INTERVIEWER: What do you mean by 'poor progress'?

ELDRA: *(speaking slowly and disappointedly)* If the truth be known, I came to realize that my folks back home kept me back. They depended and relied on me so much that I feel now that I was there for them and not for myself – I was kept back. Even though when I was writing the letters I felt I was important and useful, when I think about it now I could not even spell properly and I was making out to them that I was such a little genius. At times I just convinced myself that I could spell certain words and went about spelling words in my own sweet way and my family knew no different. I spelt particular words my way and it just stayed with me over the years – until it all caught up with me of course *(laughs)*! For years I was convinced certain words were spelt correctly – like 'dearest' which I spelt 'derest' and 'beloved' spelt 'belovered' and so many other words which I am just too ashamed to mention now. It took such a long time for me to get out of certain habits but certain words I just did not regularly come across in the books that I was reading at the time. The community gave me dictation but never confidently spelt the words for me.

INTERVIEWER: I understand that.

NARRATOR: Eldra acknowledges that she has been a victim of her own success, relied on by those who needed her but never having the opportunity to fulfil her potential.

ELDRA: Everyone came to me to write their letters and with each letter I composed I got better at producing the next one. My words would just flow on the pages with words like: 'Your kindness will be remembered with loving fondnesses' – which they mostly dictated to me. A familiar phrase was: 'I will always be indebted to you' and: 'You are always in our thoughts'. I would then add: 'We are proud to know that we have someone like you in the family, someone that we hold in such high esteem.' *(laughs)*

INTERVIEWER: So you were not taking dictation?

ELDRA: Well, yes and no. My Aunt Theresa, especially, would dictate such wonderful words, like poetry: 'My dearest and most beloved sister Eugenia', she would say, and each time I would know how to start her letters and would race ahead. There were times when I started other people's letters in the same way. For my uncle I would write: 'My dearest and most beloved brother Maurice.' If my aunt wanted money she would begin with: 'My dearest, loving and most generous brother.' *(laughs)*

INTERVIEWER: Do you think your grandmother reading to you had anything to do with the 'poor progress' you mentioned?

ELDRA: If you are asking if looking after my grandmother at such a young age also kept me back, then definitely yes, as perhaps I could have had access to wider learning opportunities, but I know I received so many benefits because my grandmother was a clever woman and she taught me so much. She used to work at the only post office in the Mountain Valley village and that was a highly important job in those days. Apart from my grandmother, I did not get an opportunity to really mix with people who could help me progress educationally. I didn't think the headmaster at the school was ever keen to see me go further with my education, not in the way that my grandmother did. She always praised me and made me feel good about myself but the headmaster did not have any interest in me and always found fault.

SCENE 2: *In search of a diploma*

INTERVIEWER: And what did you mean earlier when you referred to 'achieving educational goals'?

ELDRA: By that I mean possessing a college diploma, a recognized certificate, and to feel that I have achieved something academically speaking. Learning is what everyone wants, and which person would deny its importance? I blame my own self for not acquiring sufficient education earlier in my life, as I feel I did not do enough to get myself a decent education after my grandmother passed. I was naïve and I thought I knew it all but, when I reflect, I realize I had no choice about staying on in school. This couldn't happen today but when I was a young girl, it just seemed the right thing for the family to have me do – look after my grandmother – because I was always the one who was there for her. It was like my mother lost interest in me after my grandmother started looking after me but my mother gave my sister a chance for a good education, and for me, achieving a college diploma has always been my goal.

NARRATOR: Despite the barriers she faced in the form of family and community responsibilities, Eldra continued to blame herself for not achieving her educational goals.

INTERVIEWER: And what has prevented you from achieving this goal up until now?

ELDRA: You should know that I have not quite got my diploma yet – I am still working towards it. In modern times, while there are many opportunities to learn in adult life, when you are trying to get a significant education in later life you feel so embarrassed because you think that people think you wasted your time when you were young, and now it seems like you are just looking for a handout in some way. Education to me is like money – it is valuable, everbody wants it really – and I compare it to people in this country who look fit to work but who are taking handouts from the state. It is as if they did something wrong along the way. When they were young they wasted their time and that is the reason why they have to ask for education in adult life. In my younger adult life, I felt a little embarrassed that if I started applying for education people would judge me. I think that I was also probably worried about showing myself up and letting others see how little education I actually had. But when I was a young person in the West Indies I would say I spent my whole childhood helping others and that played a part in me not really seeing the bigger picture. I secretly wanted to become a teacher and somehow felt I was already there, and getting qualified did not even enter into the equation. I did not set myself any personal goals at the time and was too busy caring for others.

INTERVIEWER: You mean caring for your grandmother?

ELDRA: No, not just my grandmother – helping other extended family members with all sorts – and this included really basic things like writing letters. When I came to England, all I did was care for others too, and even today, I am still writing letters for former constituents.

NARRATOR: As an older black woman, Eldra's experience of caring for others in the community and supporting those 'less educated' may not be unique – indeed it appears widespread. Black women's activism, particularly in the area of education, then seems to remain invisible in the 'masculinist discourse of "race" and social change' (Mirza, 1997: 272).

INTERVIEWER: So today you are still helping others? And would you say that your learning is providing you with skills to help others?

ELDRA: No, my dear, I have always had those skills but what I learn I am always sharing with others naturally, and in fact whomever I come into contact with. I am constantly doing things for other people such as defending families, fighting library closures and such, but up until now I never ventured into a college to get myself educated. I always enjoyed and got a lot from representing people who did not have an education but for all these years when I was helping others, I could not see that at the same time, I could have been helping myself with the things that I really wanted to achieve.

INTERVIEWER: Can I go back to ask you about why you felt that your headmaster did not seem interested in seeing you further your education?

ELDRA: Now that is a long story and you have got me started so in order for me to give you a clear picture, I have to go back a long way. We were taught in a school which was just a big open-plan space, with no side rooms, and children of all ages were taught under the same roof. Sometimes there was just one teacher for the whole class and other times the headmaster would have two other teachers he had trained, who would take classes in other parts of the room. We children could see each other from all parts of the open classroom and sometimes we would hear when one of us was being told off by the headmaster. We had to try to keep really quiet so we could hear the teachers' instructions because if you did not catch the instructions, talked too much or misbehaved, you were bound to receive a lash from the headmaster. We got to do dictation a lot and the headmaster would ask us to spell words like 'contemplation' and we had to write it down. He would then ask us to spell something like 'devastation' and we would also have to write that down in our exercise book. Next he would say: 'Spell "emancipation" and spell "remembrance".' He would make sure that it was always a long word and we were sitting close to each other on the benches but we would not dare look at what the next person was writing down otherwise we would get our name called out or receive a lash from the headmaster if we were close to him.

INTERVIEWER: How did you feel about that?

ELDRA: The plain truth was each and every one of us felt each other's shame when one of us was picked on to spell the word out aloud. If you got a word wrong, a minute after Mountain Valley School ended for that day, the whole village would know already who the foolish one was and who took the shame. I was afraid of school education for a long time and was quite fearful of the headmaster and found it very hard to learn from anyone other than from my grandmother. At least when my grandmother scolded me there was no one else to see my embarrassment. I dreaded exam day at the school.

SCENE 3: Exam day stress in the British colonial education system

INTERVIEWER: Tell me about exam day.

ELDRA: On the day of an exam we children were dressed in our best clothes just as if we were going to church. The boys would have neat haircuts and we girls would have our hair neatly plaited and we would carry our slates and lead pencils to class. Exam day was very important and if you did not pass the exam you went down a class or you stayed in the same class, depending on how badly you did. There were some big tall children who had to sit in the same class as the smaller children and sometimes children would be as much as four years older than the rest of their classmates. After the exams, we never had any paper to tell us the results; the headmaster would call our name out loud and everyone could hear each other's fate. On the day the results came out, he would shout out the names of the children who did badly really loudly in a really mean way and this was carried out in front of the whole school. If you heard your name loudly you knew it was going to be bad news! The ones who passed would hear their names read out softly, gently, clear and courteously.

ELDRA continues talking without prompting from the INTERVIEWER.

ELDRA: *(quoting the headmaster)* 'Matilda Grooms! You going back to first grade!'
'Vee-ron-nee-ca Jules … you moving up to fourth grade.'
'Moo-reen De … Lancy – you are moving to fifth grade!'
'Ronald Richards! You staying where you are!'
'Winston Sommerset! You are dropping a grade!'
'Sandra Thomas! You not moving anywhere!'

INTERVIEWER: *(intervening)* How do you remember hearing your name being called out?

ELDRA: The names were usually read out in alphabetical order but not always. It was like the headmaster wanted to confuse us on occasions but he was always right and the children never dare cross him. When my name was called out very slowly in the wrong order, I did not hear the tone accurately, as the nerves got the better of me and I was just concentrating on the incorrect pronunciation.

ELDRA proceeds to relate the exchange between her and the headmaster.

ELDRA: 'El-draa Bes-sik', he said in a slow, clear soft English accent.
'Bes Wick!' I shouted back impulsively in order to correct the pronunciation of my Vincentian father's mispronounced surname.
The headmaster stared across at me for what seemed like forever and then bellowed out, 'Where is your manners child? You want to stay where you are?' he demanded, looking down and over his spectacles.
The children were trying to conceal their laughter and some of them were holding both hands over their mouths.
'No, Mr Henry,' I remembered saying.
'No what, child?' he roared.
'No, Mr Henry, I want to further my education.'
'Then you had better hush your mouth and stop your interference!' he barked, to more muffled sounds of laughter from the children.

ELDRA pauses.

ELDRA: What a scary system that was then. Can you imagine if they did it that way today? In St Lucia, if you did not pass the exam and if you did not go up a class there would be big trouble at home – you had to tell your mother and grandmother as soon as you got in because if you did not, everyone else would be telling them. I was frightened that I would not go up a class because I knew what my grandmother would say – 'You too bright for your own good.' I was expected to pass as I were one of the clever older children that the head teacher might eventually train to teach the younger children.

INTERVIEWER: How did you get on with the headmaster after that?

ELDRA: The headmaster continued to mispronounce my surname all the time I remained in his school. I just could not see past that experience and could not learn anything much after that. Even though I felt he was wrong, he would not stand to be corrected by me and I remember this experience to this day but he did eventually move me up to the next level but I never got to find out his decision until a whole week later – in his own sweet time, when he had knocked a little of the wind off of my sails.

NARRATOR: The negative experiences and humiliation meted out by male teachers have had a major impact on the educational trajectory of first-generation African Caribbean women. This impact was vividly described by Anselma in Act 1 (A Story of Reading) and also alluded to by Dorothy in Act 4 (A Story of Learning for Challenge).

ELDRA: This was very upsetting for my grandmother because while she knew I was wrong to answer back to the headmaster, she also knew that she had taught me that a person could pronounce their own name how they wished and that a person should not be told by others how they wished their name to be pronounced. Today I now know that that is the English pronouncing my surname.

INTERVIEWER: Is that so?

ELDRA: I have been hearing the 'proper pronunciation' for years now but still did not change the way I pronounced it. I never did get a chance to talk to my grandmother about my experiences with pronouncing my surname in England.

SCENE 4: *Alternative learning and preparing for the UK*

INTERVIEWER: Before your grandmother died were you actually prevented from going to school?

ELDRA: When I was 13, my grandmother got sick really bad and I had to leave school to care for her. She got better after six months and she sent me back to school as she did not want me to stay off school for too long – but then she was poorly again. Eventually she did not have any say in the matter because at times she could not always communicate and, as I had already had some bad experiences at school, I didn't really want to go back. I was not actually prevented really but there was nothing I was learning at school that I could not learn from her at home even if it was at times she taught me from her sick bed.

INTERVIEWER: So how would you describe the barriers to your learning then?

ELDRA: The truth was at a very early age getting learning inside me was a problem and getting clever people around me to teach me was a bigger problem. My grandmother was the only person around me whom I knew was clever and had a lot of time for me when I was young. After she died, my mother felt I was too outspoken and that was the reason why my education suffered. She felt that because I answered back to those in authority my education suffered greatly but I believe it was the opposite and that it was because I answered back that my education was as good as it was. I have to say that when I was very young I learned fast and I was good at remembering things but in school we read from the Crown Readers and, for us as a generation, that was often seen by some of my generation as 'indoctrination' and my sister in particular referred to it as 'brainwashing'. This could have been seen as a barrier to other learning but as a teenager a lot of the books my sister preferred were books which came from the bigger West Indian islands, like Brer Anancy from Jamaica which was all mostly fiction [see James, 2004]. I told myself, at least my grandmother was teaching me history.

INTERVIEWER: Did you go back to school after your grandmother passed away?

ELDRA: Now I am going to come clean and tell you that when my grandmother died I did not go back to school but stayed in the house looking after my sister's children and just helping others in the village.

NARRATOR: It seems that Eldra may have decided at a very early age to opt out of education and may have given up on a Caribbean education system as a direct result of her earlier negative experiences.

INTERVIEWER: Did you plan to come to the UK?

ELDRA: When I was 18, my godparents, who had been living in England for several years, contacted me with a view to me coming over to study nursing over in the UK and it was like a scholarship for learning in England. I did not really want to do nursing; I wanted to study law or something similar but, in the end, I did not really care what I would be studying – going to England was such a big opportunity. It was planned for a long time but I was unaware that my godmother had become unwell, hence the delay, so it took some time before I eventually arrived in England. They did not have any children of their own and so within a year of my arrival in the UK I ended up having to care for my godmother full-time and there was no talk of the promised nursing studies.

INTERVIEWER: So much caring for others in your life.

ELDRA: Seems like the story of my whole life but not really. I am just about to take off properly!

INTERVIEWER: How important is learning to you?

ELDRA: There was no doubt about it, for me education was the greatest passport to a good, honest life! I remember my grandmother telling me that on countless occasions and I believed her. My older sister, who got a convent education and got pregnant soon after she finished her studies, felt that education went to my head at a very young age, and when we were growing up she was always teasing me about how I took education far too seriously and that I was getting carried away with it all and no man wanted an educated woman because he would feel subservient and no woman should allow a man to feel that way.

INTERVIEWER: How would you sum up the things that have prevented you from gaining access to learning in the past?

ELDRA: It would be easy for me to say caring for others in my young life as well as caring for others in my adult life but if I was not so driven with wanting to help others I would have probably have got myself a diploma a long time ago. But then again I did not class myself as having had a good education – good enough, but not proper. My sister, on the other hand, almost completed a good, decent education but it did not take her long to get herself married and have more children. Had this been me, it would have been a blessing in disguise as I would have had the perfect excuse for not achieving my educational goals but I have no children and no husband, so what excuse do I have?

ACT 12: Reclaiming our mother's tongue: A story of learning for identity

CAST OF CHARACTERS

NARRATOR	The INTERVIEWER speaks to the audience, as an aside
INTERVIEWER	Speaks directly to the characters
ALPHENA	Aged 61, from Dominica

SCENE 1: *Approaching the centre*

It is late afternoon as the INTERVIEWER approaches the Meads Adult Community College in Filton, in the city of Meads, to conduct a one-to-one interview with ALPHENA, a graduate, who works as a community volunteer tutor. The INTERVIEWER looks at the large purpose-built building located on the edge of a number of high-rise social housing blocks.

SCENE 2: *Advertising learning opportunities*

Before entering the community college building, the INTERVIEWER pauses to observe the leaflets posted on the display boards in the windows: 'Skills for life', 'Fitness and hospitality', 'Introduction to child minding', 'Arts and Crafts', 'Starting a new career', 'First steps to counselling in the community', 'Building employability skills'. Among the small list of language courses, her eye is drawn to a course entitled: 'French Creole patois for beginners'.

SCENE 3: *Waiting to interview*

As the INTERVIEWER sits in the reception area waiting to be collected, she cannot help but overhear a rather loud telephone conversation being conducted by a woman on a mobile phone who is sitting in the coffee area to the far left of the reception.

SCENE 4: *Drama before interview*

ALPHENA: She think she can come and make commess here, talk labrish and disrespect the project.

The spoken expressions are familiar to the INTERVIEWER.

ALPHENA: So what you saying to me sister?

The smartly dressed freckle-faced light-skinned black woman is sporting a natural afro. She walks toward the researcher as she continues with her mobile phone conversation.

ALPHENA: *(in a loud and assertive voice)* I know you are not going to go there. Hello, hello. Excuse me, excuse me. *(repeating)*

As she walks toward the INTERVIEWER, she peers at her disapprovingly as though making a judgement of her character, and continues with her conversation.

ALPHENA: What are you implying?

ALPHENA turns her back on the INTERVIEWER and turns around again, motioning her to take a seat where she had previously been sitting. The INTERVIEWER sits down and ALPHENA continues her conversation, moving the phone from one ear to the other, her silver metallic bracelets jingling together at each hurried turn.

NARRATOR: I wondered about what I was witnessing and the attitude of the woman I was about to interview. Why was she continuing with her conversation and observing me in that manner? I was also observing her and possibly prejudging her intentions. Corbin and Strauss (2008) suggest that observations have a lot to offer the qualitative researcher, and from her telephone conversation I had already recorded interesting reflections about her likely attitude to the project she was leading. However, these authors also note that the researcher may attribute incorrect meaning to an interaction without subsequently checking it out with the participants (2008: 30).

SCENE 5: *Confrontational welcome*

ALPHENA: Sorry about that. I am Alphena. You don't mind if we meet out here do you? The outreach staff are using the office and the training rooms are all booked out.

INTERVIEWER: I am grateful for your time.

ALPHENA: That name? Are you from Dominica or St Lucia?

INTERVIEWER: No, my mother is St Lucian and my father …

ALPHENA: Well that makes you St Lucian – why you have to say your mother is St Lucian?! You should be proud of your heritage and your identity!

The INTERVIEWER feels confronted – the interview is commencing in an uncomfortable manner for her.

ALPHENA: Sorry to have to say this but that is the thing about us. We don't seem to be proud of our identity. We like to forget our roots.

INTERVIEWER: I didn't mean to come across that way.

ALPHENA: You speak patois?

The INTERVIEWER feels confronted again. ALPHENA responds with another question before she can reply.

ALPHENA: *(shouting at the top of her voice, the familiar St Lucian/ Dominican greeting)* SAKAFET?

INTERVIEWER: No I don't but …

ALPHENA: I thought as much.

INTERVIEWER: My parents did not speak patois in the home …

ALPHENA interrupts again and the INTERVIEWER is prevented from speaking further.

ALPHENA: I suppose you going to tell me that they thought it would interfere in your English education! Ha ha ha.

INTERVIEWER: *(attempting to acquiesce)* You know! *(appears amused)*

ALPHENA: You know why I have to rough you up like that, don't you? I was a rebel when I was young and I did not see the point of education. I am still a rebel now, but for the right reasons.

INTERVIEWER: Of course and you are right.

ALPHENA: You know you could have learnt it?

INTERVIEWER: Learnt?

ALPHENA: Patois.

INTERVIEWER: I know. Yes I do see it as a missed opportunity.

ALPHENA: Precisely!

INTERVIEWER: *(beginning to feel concerned and worried about who is actually being interviewed and attempting to gain control of the process)* This is why your project I think is an important one. Tell me about it.

ALPHENA: You know it's never too late to learn. We have a language which is slowly dying because our parents failed to see its significance, especially those misguided parents who came to build up this big country. Those – like your parents who did not appreciate their roots and culture – those who were ashamed of their heritage.

INTERVIEWER: *(appearing visibly uncomfortable)* Misguided perhaps but surely not ashamed.

ALPHENA: Yes. Ashamed. My father is a Dominican and my mother was from St Lucia and she would Mamaguise me all the time to turn me away from speaking patois. But growing up I know it was part of my identity and made sure patois was part of my vocabulary. It never left me. In fact I cannot understand how so many St Lucian and Dominican children cannot speak patois and so many others can? It is like there is this big divide. I think those who don't speak it look down their noses at those who do speak it – as if they are better than those who speak the language. Far from it, I say!

INTERVIEWER: Well I certainly do not fit into that category. Rather the opposite *(feeling a sense of losing control)*. I agree it should be promoted and regret not being able to speak it myself.

ALPHENA: *(staring at the INTERVIEWER)* Anyway I don't want to offend you. That is not my role. You have come to ask me about lifelong learning.

INTERVIEWER: You know I am really inspired by your work. I think it is an important project. Can I start by asking you what you think of the concept of lifelong learning?

ALPHENA: Sorry for putting you on the spot but that is just my style. *(laughs out loud)*

SCENE 6: *Learning, awareness and responsibility*

INTERVIEWER: So you are learning and promoting awareness while you are delivering this course?

ALPHENA: *(pauses and takes a deep breath)* I was just a child when I came here and my mum used to say, you have to do well in your education, they have the best schools here in Great Britain and you have to do well. But she did not know what I had to put up with back then. I had a hard job defending myself in that school. I have a hard job now – but now, I able to defend my community by going back to school!

INTERVIEWER: 'Defending the community?'

ALPHENA: Yes – lifelong learning is good for defending the community. The community needs defending. I have just finished doing a degree at City Central University and I do hourly paid teaching on the Sociology module and you know on one occasion when I was giving coursework feedback to a young white student, you know what she said to me?

INTERVIEWER: Please tell me.

ALPHENA: She said, 'I feel uncomfortable about the way black students always harp on about racism. And as for slavery, they could have had the brains to do what we did. Why didn't they?' *(looks at the INTERVIEWER blankly)*

INTERVIEWER: What did you say?

ALPHENA: What could I say? I wanted to say 'perhaps there are those who are born with purity in their hearts and there are those born with evil hatred. It is not about colour' – but what could I say?

INTERVIEWER: Indeed.

ALPHENA: But you see what we are dealing with and what responsibility we have. That's what I mean about defending our community. I am still learning and I enjoy learning now – I can see its purpose.

INTERVIEWER: That is all very revealing.

NARRATOR: I wondered why she had presented her story in this way and whether it was because she wanted to give an explanation as to why she had perhaps prejudged me. I reflected on Earthy and Cronin's (2008) assertion that a narrative approach concerns not only the story-telling components or characteristics but also the social interactions between interviewer and interviewee.

ALPHENA: I am doing so much learning now at this college. I get a lot of valuable information from the High Commission and can see the progress that the islands are making to promote French Caribbean patois. You know, it is not encouraged back home at all. Not really. In fact, in most cases it is frowned-upon and considered a retrograde step. But it is such an important part of our culture. There are some in the government who would want to get rid of it but some want it as part of the curriculum. Over here we have to promote it. We are best placed to promote it because we are supposed to be more educated as we have access to so much more opportunities in the community to learn.

INTERVIEWER: But this is a voluntary initiative?

ALPHENA: *(hands the interviewer a leaflet entitled 'St Lucian Creole patois')* There is another leaflet for Dominican Creole patois but it's the same thing. Some people think it is not a proper language and that it is not written down – but look. This is an example of how it is being developed and promoted.

SCENE 7: Believing in the learning process

INTERVIEWER: What types of people come to your course?

ALPHENA: Well, I am trying to promote it in the community. I want the women to take the project seriously. I still have to get them to believe in the project. It is not easy when their parents gave them this negative view that the language is inferior. In this area there is a large West Indian community and of course it is the area with the most Dominicans and St Lucians. I am looking at learning for the younger generation but there is a lot of work to do.

NARRATOR: At the end of the interview, I was relaxed and comfortable. I concluded that Alphena's apparent rudeness was a result of a combination of frustration and anticipation. On the one hand, it was clear that she had a passion for her project, but also that she had doubts about the commitment of the other women in helping her bring it to fruition. (I recalled her opening statement via the mobile phone conversation: 'She think she can come and make commess here, talk labrish and disrespect the project'.) This implied that there may be challenges over the ways in which the older women worked together to achieve their immediate learning goals.

Alphena was eager to share with me the uniqueness of the project as a lifelong learning initiative but she was concerned about the future as some of the women appeared not to be taking it seriously.

NARRATOR: The woman being interviewed has a great deal to say and she continues.

Chapter 8

Towards a policy for matriarchal learning hubs

In this study I observed that older black women gained support and confidence from other women and from the sense and strength of belonging they derived, they were able to help tackle and respond to problems in their communities. As Colley *et al.* (2002: 1) noted: 'We cannot learn without belonging (to something) and we cannot belong without learning the practices, norms, values and understandings of the community that we belong to.' While this reflexive understanding of lifelong learning as belonging is visible from the narratives, many of the women in my study also experienced competing tensions because they were learning and promoting change together.

Lifelong learning for older black women is therefore, I believe, part-emancipator and part-purposefully responsible learning. It can take the form, as cited in the women's stories, of learning to improve the health of the community or supporting communities affected by serious issues such as black-on-black gun crime. In all such circumstances, a form of matriarchal learning can occur, for example on the social housing estate, where older black mothers appreciate the collective sense of social responsibility and desire to share knowledge that helps generate the confidence to tackle major community concerns. It can be said that older black women are beginning to re-consider a lost role beyond the home, and in parallel with the studies of their white contemporaries (Etienne and Jackson, 2011), learning becomes a vital prerequisite and integral part of encouraging meaningful participation and active citizenship. My study has revealed that lifelong learning has a strong connection with emancipation, and in view of the growing population of black elders faced with reduced welfare and community facilities, 'an emancipatory approach to lifelong learning is perhaps more needed than ever' (Biesta, 2012: 6).

As a result of previous humiliation and shame experienced in earlier educational contexts, as the women's educational stories have amply demonstrated, independence and control over learning were crucial factors for first-generation African Caribbean women to experience positive learning in community settings. The study illustrated the importance of learning in later years for the women's development and wellbeing but it also demonstrated its wider emancipatory role in redressing past injustices and potentially tackling future ones as the women found new confidence and shared their awareness and critical perceptions more widely and with younger generations. Older black women learners in the study have shown that they can free themselves of past learning barriers to influence and learn in partnership with others within self-constructed communities of practice where, as a result of their shared ethnic and cultural heritage, they can excel together as learners, affecting their own and others' emancipation. The women in my study were learning together with their own agendas, taking charge as they made decisions on what they wanted to learn and what they needed to know, as part of a newly emancipated, empowered group of learning elders. From marginalized and alienated experiences of education and schooling, they had discovered and created – and were further motivated by – the emancipatory potential of informal learning spaces.

Ultimately my research sought to explore the benefits of lifelong learning by examining how older black women promoted learning via interactions with each other in informal learning settings, enabling polyrhythmic realties to emerge. My research adopted a black feminist lens for contemporary narrative study of the benefits of learning for black Caribbean mothers and daughters who returned to the UK motherland as immigrants and experienced this learning in their later years. To judge from the stories of older black women in the study, learning was often synonymous with both respect and community (Hoggett, 1997), as well as being about redressing past losses – justifying the particular lens assumed. Although the research acknowledged the critical struggles of the black male in UK society, it chose to hear only the narratives of older black women as a means to understand the educational experiences of a largely unheard group of older learners. The insights these women provide also shed light on a wider community of learners and the interrelated experiences of identity, learning, community, voluntary action and mechanisms for social change.

By combining the study of learning and community in particular areas, the reflexive and complex nature of these two ideas, interwoven with cultural and learner identities, could be explored. The participants were seen to take charge of their own learning activities, bringing the community challenges into their personal and learning lives and into their homes. In this way matriarchal learning hubs developed from the women learning in womanist ways, where the learning spaces inspired new confidence to flourish.

Matriarchal learning hubs where polyrhythmic realities occurred fostered opportunities for learning to progress, as the women passed on learning from their classes and formal associations to other sisters. In such settings the older women took responsibility for the development of their own, sometimes 'alternative', approaches to learning, with narratives revealing a sense of achievement and respect for life and the wider community. Far from a lifelong learning model designed to instil skills, older black women appeared not to require public services to learn, but were keen to bring and share their own experiences and skills. However, they were clearly dependent on support from the state to make such community learning spaces, and sometimes facilitators, available to them.

Image and text courtesy of Looshan Saltfish

Figure 9: Ma Lejay – 'Learning and cursing keeps us living. It is right that we argue about the price of fish'

Future policy and research: Learning for wellbeing in an ageing, multi-cultural society

In the sections that follow I reflect critically on my research, examining its strengths and limitations, and consider needs for further research and future policy for learning for elders in multicultural urban settings.

My findings highlight the significance of informal learning settings for older black women, revealing the connections between volunteering and learning activities. Many of the women in the study experienced a particular sense of responsibility in their desire to use their learning for the benefit of others and toward community changes. Among the strengths of the study was the methodological approach that gave voice to a previously under-represented group in the literature, weaving together past and present experiences with future aspirations. The women participants' deep interest in learning in their later years invariably emanated from a past, often shared, history of learning denials, humiliation and missed opportunities. The vast majority of the women had learnt (been taught) from within a rigid colonial education system. Other, slightly younger, first-generation African Caribbean women in the study had experienced failure in a British education system where they faced racism as young commonwealth immigrants from the British West Indies. Many of these first-generation African Caribbean women rebelled and found themselves outside the education system, but those who managed to remain appeared not to have achieved their aspirations of accessing higher levels of learning.

In contemporary settings, the women were learning together, following their own agendas and taking charge as they made decisions on what they wanted to learn and what they needed to know. They are part of a newly emancipated, empowered group of learning elders. Independence and control over learning thus became the important difference enabled in lifelong learning settings, whereas prior educational contexts had denied such independence or control. The study illustrated not only the importance of learning in later years for older black women but also its wider emancipatory potential in redressing past injustices and potentially tackling future ones.

A particular strength of the study was the wealth of data gathered from some one hundred participants across a wide range of urban areas of the UK. These data not only provided diverse, rich and vibrant stories but they also enabled me to identify some common patterns. However, this made the task of selecting which accounts to include harder, and there are many voices whose narratives could have opened up different tracks in the research.

A further strength in the research, made possible by its focus on contemporary narrative study, allowed me to capture the nuances of older black women's voices, their hopes, anxieties and frustrations – social and educational – and longed-for personal learning desires. In particular, the presentation of multiple narratives exposed the many facets of liberation enabled through the learning settings, with women building trust and supporting each other together as they challenged past and present oppositions to their advancement in their efforts to progress as sisters in the struggle. This approach to gathering and rendering data also showed the different ways in which women passed on their knowledge and how they situated their learning and established varied communities of practice where they could appreciate the benefits of their learning.

These reflections on different community environments and the meanings each group of women took from them also revealed how their polyrhythmic learning realities flourished. There is also wider relevance from recognizing the positive kinds of learning experiences presented here, in that community-learning environments can be replicated across many multi-racial communities and the benefits extended across communities. The seemingly 'natural' evolution of informal learning practices, which proved positive in strengthening bonds and social commitment for these first-generation Caribbean women in their later years, offers lessons for the value of informal learning for social wellbeing and promoting cohesive bonds more widely. Similarly, the strong connections between learning and volunteer activities could have wider policy relevance. Linking the idea of matriarchal (and community) learning hubs developed from my findings to existing strategies for older people's learning appears significant in promoting the wellbeing of older learners in multi-cultural settings – yet these kinds of 'non-essential' facilities are diminishing rapidly. Away from more formal learning settings and external facilitators, the women have a chance to be themselves 'alone and together', as lifelong learners in a struggle to remain active, motivated and useful members of society as they age.

Limitations and implications for further research

A particular limitation in the research was the absence of a voice from others – from the wider community – on the impact of the women's learning. It was beyond the scope of this study to investigate the extent to which members of the wider community acknowledged this impact.

In addition, this empirical study, while exploring the benefits of learning, could have delved deeper into the precise nature of learning for black women as well as men in tackling concerns in the community such as youth violence. For many of the older black woman learners and community volunteers, learning later in life appeared not just to be about personal development, enjoyment or acquiring a qualification but, as previously stated, about the achieving of a 'badge of honour'. In the minds of the women, this would send out a clear signal to the rest of their community, garnering respect on both sides. For the women, that signalled honour, emancipation and pride in overcoming a challenge. Learning was also valued as a source of strength, which they gained from working alongside others in the wider community.

My analysis suggests that feelings of 'representing' others or learning for the community were present in the minds of the women participants but there was little scope in the study to examine the extent to which this was acknowledged or perceived by those outside these groups of women. The narrative depth of the study inevitably restricted this kind of breadth.

Research with members of the wider communities surrounding the women participants and exploration of their perceptions of the roles carried out by the women may have offered additional insights into the benefits of these learning settings for preventing isolation and social exclusion, such as on local housing estates. The nature of social capital for older black men was also missing from this research and this is a priority area for future research.

Another potential limitation of the research is that it focused on just one ethnic group – namely, African Caribbean – and this could be considered a weakness as the learning needs of other older ethnic groups are equally important and similarly under-researched. However, the depth of research with one group in the population is also a particular strength, as the empirical study focused on the views of women who had shared cultural experiences of immigration at a particular period in time. This allowed me to select participants with this background and to explore and compare the benefits of their learning, allowing for a detailed focus and for narratives to be explored in depth. If the views of other (or all) ethnic groups on the impact of older women's learning had been considered, the responses may have been different, but the primary focus of the research and its approach would have shifted. If members of the wider local population had been asked similar questions, their prior experiences of learning would have been more diverse and shaped by different language and cultural experiences. This would clearly be a significant extension of the current study and represents further research that needs to be addressed.

What the book reveals

I conclude that as a result of the nature of their social interactions in community settings, first-generation African Caribbean women are able to achieve benefits from lifelong learning both for themselves and for their wider communities. I have considered the nature of participation in lifelong learning and highlighted a number of barriers faced by the women in accessing learning. The theatrical acts illustrated the various learning opportunities they experienced. In summary this book:

- exposes the nature of contemporary black feminist (womanist) voices among older lifelong learning communities in UK cities
- demonstrates the extent and benefits of unity, trust and solidarity in first-generation African Caribbean women's informal learning communities
- introduces a new concept – black matriarchal learning hubs – extending the idea of learning from social participation and depicting the benefits of lifelong learning in gendered, social and cultural settings
- introduces a further new concept – dramatized annotated narratives – where the narratives of research participants are laid out as theatrical scripts and discussed by a narrator
- illustrates older black women learners' aspirations to develop their learning and education for supporting others in the wider community
- reveals the nature of practical commitment to promoting lifelong learning for social justice among UK first-generation African Caribbean women, highlighting the power of shared learning in promoting social change
- provides rich new cultural insights into the nature of lifelong learning among older black women.

Linking the beginning and the end

It is clear from the voices of the women who took part in this study how significant their learning activities have been for them in their later years, not least in addressing their long absence from educational participation and wider social participation.

In my review of the mainly African American feminist literature but also black British and black Caribbean feminist epistemology in Chapter 3, I highlight a natural tendency for older black women to nurture and support the extended black community. It was clear that the majority of the women in the study were living and interacting with others in socially deprived settings. They experienced greater social concerns, such as the effects of crime in their locality and the impact of poor education. In such circumstances, however, the women shared a desire to learn for the betterment of these communities, thereby nurturing but also promoting enhanced knowledge and power among the black community.

This book has explored the conceptual and theoretical issues surrounding two major debates in approaches to lifelong learning (Chapter 5): on the one hand, a debate prioritizing an inclusive social dimension to lifelong learning; and, on the other hand, a government-favoured, economic imperative. This latter dimension focused on achieving paid employment while neglecting learning pathways involving social purposes and general wellbeing. The literature reveals a major problem here. While previous lifelong learning studies demonstrated its significant benefits for older people, and women in particular, they appeared not to include older black women – who were largely invisible in the discourse. In an increasingly ageing society, this could be construed as a major anomaly as policies should, both in theory and practice, take steps to pursue the needs of all sections of the population. The chapter examined the important benefits of learning in later years – not least for wellbeing, friendships and combating isolation – and acknowledged the absence of discussion on minority ethnic communities. Again my findings highlighted the benefits of informal social learning contexts for black women elders, supporting but also adding to the literature by highlighting the interconnectedness of learning and voluntary social action.

I revisited the women's stories when analysing black feminist theories in education in the UK and recognized my connection as a 'sister in the struggle'. I identified collective understandings, differences and similarities in approaches to education and learning across the African Caribbean diaspora. The older black women's struggles in public-sector-led urban regeneration initiatives offered insights into how power is played out (Foucault, 1980: 82). In such circumstances, however, the women are employing their new skills to transport them from the margins to the centre and from invisibility to visibility as their views are taken on board.

Inside the discursive informal learning environments, the women communicated in their confident polyrhythmic learning realities – the structures of which are embedded in the various narrative asides in the different acts. Chapters 2, 4 and 6 revealed the extent to which particular groups of older black women engaged actively as citizens, visible elders and learners in their communities. Illustrated in these chapters were the women's successes in overcoming obstacles to their learning so they might become 'powerful outsiders' while maintaining a role as significant 'insiders' (Hoggett, 1997) too, with the ability to influence change at local level.

In their project membership, officer or board member roles, we saw the significance of learning in moving the women from the position of novices to 'experts'. This transition was emancipatory. They moved to engage in legitimate peripheral participation (Lave, 2001), able to benefit from their learning thanks to their growing empowerment both inside and outside the projects. On reflection I found that, despite sharing the same ethnic heritage, I too had experienced this duality of roles in the research process as an outsider and insider. I was often openly challenged by the women but also welcomed and embraced by them as a 'sister in the struggle'.

The various acts highlighted the valuable role that learning played in the lives of older black women in these UK settings and showed that learning in the third and fourth ages has potentially significant benefits for a group typically susceptible to high levels of illness. The Acts highlighted the polyrhythmic nature of learning that can be passed on from mothers to daughters, and pointed to the benefits of such learning in helping to improve the lives of the women and those of others in the communities around them.

Lifelong learning: The economic dimensions

Learning strategies related to economic and employment outcomes predominate in policy documents, at the expense of informal learning. This lack is reflected in national targets for educational participation, and hence is readily discounted by all of us as immeasurable (Gorard, 2000). Sadly, in a society dominated by free market economy, effective education and welfare policies cannot be developed (Griffin, 2000). Markets reinforce and reproduce inequalities (ibid.: 5). Yet it is clear that many of those seeking to learn later in life include first-generation African Caribbean women and many others who aspire to learn for non-economic reasons.

The lack of a voice for black women is a major omission in the trend of policies to seek to address growing social exclusion (McNair, 2009) and improve citizenship and community cohesion. Informal learning is an important model for meeting the personal educational desires of black women and in sharing activities and responsibilities in local community settings. The NIACE (2007) inquiry, along with Jackson's (2007) work on lifelong learning, stress the importance of social participation as integral to learning and note the lack of detailed study of the different groups of older learners. Specifically in the context of an ageing black Caribbean population, there is still a great deal more to explore, not least the benefits of such learning to the wider population. The following and final act in the book illustrates the loneliness feared by one black woman as she approaches retirement and reflects on her learning. This act is in stark contrast to the other stories of learning so far depicted in this book. The woman being interviewed had hoped to locate friends from her membership of a once-active black women's group to participate in a joint interview with me. However, lack of contact meant this was not possible. She agreed to be interviewed alone.

Loss of a stable community venue had resulted in the demise of the group. The woman about to be interviewed now taught part-time on a university 'widening access' programme located in the city centre. Despite being busy teaching in her later years, she yearned for the company of other black women of her generation.

ACT 13: 'Reaching self-actualization?': Roxanne's story

CAST OF CHARACTERS

NARRATOR	The INTERVIEWER speaks to the audience, as an aside
INTERVIEWER	Speaks directly to the characters
ROXANNE	Aged 57, from Guyana

SCENE 1: *An interview before class*

The INTERVIEWER enters a quiet room in the annexe of a higher education college. She is about to interview a black woman of mixed Asian and African Caribbean heritage.

ROXANNE: I've been in London for fifty years. I arrived in 1960. When we first came to Manchester we lived with my uncle and he had four children already and my other aunt had two, so that meant there were eight youngsters as well as the mums and dads.

INTERVIEWER: How did you come to be in London?

ROXANNE: My dad couldn't find work in Manchester so he come to get a job in London. We packed up and came down – I think he came down first and almost found a job straight away in a plastics factory.

ROXANNE is smiling and relaxed as she looks at the INTERVIEWER. Bright sunshine from the large window lights up her face as she tells her story.

ROXANNE: We got thrown out of a flat once *(laughs)*. We never really knew what the reasons were but it was probably because they didn't want us children. *(continues laughing as she reminisces about her childhood)*

SCENE 2: *Learning and surviving racism*

INTERVIEWER: So about your learning?

ROXANNE: I think, for me, my learning started, in my memory, at primary school. The fact that I was already aware at that time that I was way ahead of the kids academically says a great deal. I knew all the answers to everything and I started getting bullied because of that. At that time I used to get a lot of racist abuse too. So you then start to back down a bit. You don't say so much and of course your ability to learn any more is really messed up.

INTERVIEWER: You were way ahead of the other children? Tell me more.

ROXANNE: Well yes. I used to say to myself, 'When is the class going to start?' and then realize that the class was already happening *(laughs)*. I thought, this is great. No hard work here! Back home they were really strict about education and here it was all fun.

INTERVIEWER: So you experienced bullying back then. How did you cope? How did it impact on your learning?

ROXANNE: The thing I learnt that was one way of surviving the racism I faced was telling the other kids stories about elephants or tigers. It did not matter that I had never ever seen one in my life *(laughs)*! But that distracted them. It stopped them from thinking of beating up on me.

INTERVIEWER: What did you learn from that?

ROXANNE: I learnt what the English were like back then – from the pain I felt when the neighbour's child was not allowed to play with me and getting into fights on the street. Then going to secondary school and really not functioning at all but being very naughty. But this was really about me learning that how really I was not part of the society – I was an outsider.

INTERVIEWER: How did you cope?

ROXANNE: I created my own little project: I set up my own little library. I only had one book in it but I took it round to all the black children in the neighbourhood and asked them if they wanted to borrow it. They filled out little cards. That was so much fun back then!

ROXANNE appears relaxed and is smiling as she reflects on her project.

INTERVIEWER: Interesting.

ROXANNE: I also got tough on the streets back then and learnt how to deal with the gangs because in those days there were a lot of white gangs and if you didn't belong to a gang, you got beaten up and even if you belonged to a gang you still got beaten up by members of your own gang because you were black! But I had to tolerate that in order to fit in.

INTERVIEWER: My word!

ROXANNE: And then I left school at 15 and did various casual jobs and eventually ended up working for a legal department as a clerk – a filing clerk – and they promoted me very rapidly but my real sense of my learning development came when they started to use legal words that I didn't understand and I thought, 'I've got to get an education.'

INTERVIEWER: I see.

ROXANNE: They'd send me to the high courts with a message for the barristers and I could not understand what the messages meant. I thought, 'What are they talking about?' That's when I thought I am too illiterate; I have to get a formal education. That came four years later. I had been hanging around doing little jobs and learning to type and things in order to get on but I didn't have a formal education up until I was 21. Today at age 57 I work as a part-time hourly paid tutor.

INTERVIEWER: Part-time lecturing?

ROXANNE: Yes, and my previous learning – informal learning, that is – comes through voluntary activities over years, you know, black women's movement. I was very active in the 80s in the community – doing all sorts of things. My lifelong learning comes from being a community activist over the years but I feel I have been washed up on a shore at the moment and I think what do I want to do next and what do I want to start learning? Yes something different. But I feel quite alone now.

SCENE 3: *Missing interactions with black sisters*

ROXANNE: I think at a political and spiritual level, with the women I grew up with in London, we share a similar history. I think we are all still learning, but you know many like me have retreated back into their families, caring for them, and as a result we are not involved in community work in groups anymore. I miss the interactions in black women's groups. We need that to still keep us going. I am aware of black women my age who have burnt themselves out and have faced breakdowns and this is as a result of the pressures and stresses we have faced over the years. Our parents did not get it growing up as children – they had it when they were adults and they were able to cope with it better, I think. But we may be coming to an end of it now. I think I have noticed that in the last ten years.

Image and text courtesy of Jean Ju Pierre

Figure 10: Jean – 'I am now learning photography and I am having the best time ever'

INTERVIEWER: So you miss the interaction with other black women?

ROXANNE: So much. I think we have arrived at a new point of energy at this stage in our lives – almost like a new peace – and we look at our lives differently. I feel in a way I have got my degrees and I have probably reached self-actualization but I know right now I would like to be talking to more women of my generation. I feel it is important and there is more we can do but in a different way.

INTERVIEWER: What do you mean by 'different'?

ROXANNE: I think we are definitely learning differently now. None of the pressures of other stuff exists at this time. But I think we are isolated – from each other. This was largely out of choice before but we have now lost all the networks. We have gone inwards and it's different now. Now we have the time to do it we don't know where we are. We can't find each other. We don't really know how to find each other. Maybe we do not have the will anymore. It is a shame because I must admit I do long for the sisterly chats we used to have together.

INTERVIEWER: In what ways are we learning differently now?

ROXANNE: You know, reading books, talking about what we've read, passing books on to each other. I really miss passing on ideas. I feel we have lost something – being part of something. I would really like us all to have a sense of what's happening to us now. Sometimes I think, rightly or wrongly, that our mothers had an easier time than us. They are living longer and, though they had stress, it was a different time of stress and not as sustained as what we experienced. At least when they turned 60 they could start up again, really enjoy life. Now we have to wait till we are 65 to retire. But I am not tired *(laughs out loud)*. Right now I do want to go out and socialize with other women and I like the idea of just sitting and chatting. But we do not have regular places for people of my age – it's either too young for us or too old for us.

SCENE 4: *Revival of the life and soul of the black woman*

ROXANNE: *(looking pensive as she continues to reflect)* A lot of women started to have children, women I never expected to have children. They got married, which was quite a shock, given they were feminist and very adamant about their sexuality. So a lot of women who felt they were lesbians suddenly were pregnant with children and that was quite a shock. This is a real shame for those of us who stuck to our guns. They really let the side down.

INTERVIEWER: In what way?

ROXANNE: When you think of the struggles that we went through and the struggles that I have been through in the last 50 years and the hopes that you had for younger black women and we are still being pushed into sport, music, pushed into fashion, pushed into dance – you know it really makes me angry.

INTERVIEWER: What's wrong with these?

ROXANNE: Well, when I know some of these young people are capable of being mathematicians or architects or lawyers and doctors and we haven't got there yet. I talk to these young women who are having children and it's about awareness and it would be interesting to see what happens to their children when they go to school, because they are not going to take it the way we did.

INTERVIEWER: And what about this current generation – fourth generation?

ROXANNE: Our grandchildren are putting up with a lot but I don't think they realize how hard we tried. Their mothers are the children of these radical women who were really gearing them up to face some tough times. With Obama now, there is massive hope that these children will make something of themselves – particularly the boy children. I am very angry that you can't live in a community without being harassed still. It's the same old thing, nothing's changed. It's still there but we are flattened trying to fight against it. My closest friend is my neighbour and the two of us have formed an alliance for protection from continued harassment from our neighbours.

INTERVIEWER: The struggle goes on.

Review of Act 13

Roxanne's story reveals the urgency for black matriarchal learning hubs to maintain, and at times revive, the life and soul of older black women. The need for social and political activism in social networks appears to be ever more necessary in the older black womanist community.

Beyond the scope of this book, however, are the experiences of the many older African Caribbean and other black people who are not engaged in community-based volunteering and learning. There are unanswered questions relating to the comparative nature of their lives and wellbeing. The stories of the vast majority of women in this book evolved in their collective matriarchal learning hubs, and these at times proved effective and powerful ways of progressing their learning lives. Those away from these matriarchal learning hubs yearned for sisterly involvement and co-operation.

Final reflections

This book has reflected the polyrhythmic realities reflected in the aesthetic essence of African cultures and language (Sheared, 1999: 5). Such realities afford access to perceptions at different levels, allowing for deeper understanding and knowing of others at the 'heart of the race' (Bryan *et al.*, 1985). These insights are found embedded in the stories told and in the behaviours, attitudes and actions of the participants in my study. Starting from the concept of polyrhythmic realities allowed me to capture the multiple rhythms (Sheared, 1999) flowing through the women's discussions within their various social and cultural learning settings. For example, in my questions around the nature and benefits of learning, the particular ways in which the women held their discussions – openly talking about, and telling tales about, each other – and the nature of sisterly sparring evident in their conversations – at times encouraging but at times critical – offered insights into their gains and ways of engaging in informal learning communities.

The polyrhythmic realities were reflected in the swift emotional transitions from sadness and upset to happiness and hope and in the constant interruptions and impatient talking across each other. And the triviality with which they addressed apparently significant issues similarly displayed the manifestations of informal learning inside black matriarchal learning hubs. The context and social interactions, as much as the focus or subject of the learning they discussed, were clearly embedded in their experiences of what they described as learning. The subjects they identified as the focus of learning were also significant and linked to understandings of prior learning, histories and Caribbean cultural settings.

Black matriarchs and the inadequacies of categorization

Identity was an important feature of this book. The black women matriarchs in the first act were adamant about wanting to be identified as West Indians. Informal learning in their later years seemed to have imbued them with new confidence, providing the much-needed vehicle that enabled them to openly voice their opinions. There are conflicting conceptions of what it means to be older, black and female in the UK, and the women's stories argue the need for further exploration of critical race theory (Rollock, 2011; Gillborn, 2006) and the acceptance or otherwise of labels seemingly forced on older black British communities based on American conceptions.

The women appeared undaunted, however, by externally imposed labels, and asserted a clear choice in separating African from Caribbean. This choice seemed critical to their symbolic identities. They had already directly experienced what it meant to be labelled as coloured, and then black ... but now African? While, at one level, they appeared accepting of earlier labels, their stories indicate the extent of their discomfort with these externally imposed designations. In their later years they demonstrated a new confidence, drawn from their shared community learning, which endowed them with the strength to assert their deeply felt preferences around their own labels of identity. The term 'African Caribbean' was a new and unwelcome label the women were unwilling to accept.

Their insistence on a self-selected label symbolizes other resistances in the nature of their learning, such as unwillingness to compromise on the content of the learning material or certain approaches, and even how they challenged my attempts to get them to focus on my questions. They associated being inappropriately labelled 'African Caribbean' in a world where services often failed to meet their needs appropriately with further exclusion of their distinct West Indian histories, and therefore feared that ultimately their contributions would go unrecognized. Stuart Hall captures these sentiments thus:

> *When I was growing up in the 1940s and 1950s as a child in Kingston, I was surrounded by the signs, music and rhythms of this Africa of the Diaspora, which only existed as a result of a long and discontinuous series of transformations. But, although almost everyone around me was some shade of brown or black (Africa 'speaks'!), I never once heard a single person refer to themselves or to others as, in some way, or as having been at some time in the past, 'African'.*

(Hall, 1992: 231)

The narrative stories depicted in Act 2 featured women who probably depended chiefly on social housing, health and social care support, in contrast with the women leading materially comfortable lives featured in Act 3, who had greater confidence and independence. However, by the nature of their volunteering the women presented in this chapter show their shared belief in the value of education and learning, and their commitment to community endeavour and volunteering for the benefit of others.

In Act 1 we saw how even *possessing* a book was a symbol of education, and signalled its importance. However, that the book was carried about unread and that the shame of being unable to read it remained hidden for years also underlines the damaging effects of being denied access to learning at a young age. Black women who are learning late in life are faced with, and have to come to terms with, many realities. These women reflect on missed opportunities, their hopes for their children, their aspirations and the learning journeys still to come. My understanding of their behaviour, attitudes to learning and awareness of its benefits is grounded in my own experience of learning.

On my first visit to meet the participants in this research (Act 1, Meads), I was concerned about what seemed to be a rather rude welcome from one of the women but, in hindsight, it was to be expected. It was Black History month and there was much looking back to the days of the empire and slavery. As they told me, learning and education needed to encompass wider aspirations about the present and future as well as the past. As the first two acts show, poverty and related welfare concerns remain a feature of the lives of many first-generation African Caribbean women in the UK but also of their lives prior to arriving in the 1950s and 1960s. As examined in Chapter 3, education, including lifelong learning, has been closely connected with social mobility and economic gain. But my interviews in Acts 1 and 2, while affording glimpses of existing tensions and frustrations among black youth – these women's children and grandchildren – also suggest that benefits from learning were primarily focused around personal development. Yet there were also many indications that the women regarded their learning as making wider connections and bringing about change for the particular groups they were interacting with.

In Chapter 1, I discussed the conceptual diversity of lifelong learning and its association with continual personal development. Here I explore such development and diversity in the learning lives of three first-generation African Caribbean women who are participating in formal learning in UK colleges. These students come together in their volunteering roles as community mentors but are also enrolled in formal learning programmes in Lincolnvale City. The chapter then takes a new turn, telling the stories of three older black women who are working to complete a college diploma for a specific purpose. Vereen (aged 52) is seeking to obtain a diploma to help 'empower others'; Candace (aged 54) is learning to be able to help 'raise self-esteem in the community'; and Eldra (aged 70) is studying for a diploma 'to tackle social injustice'. Just like the women learning in informal settings, they too appear to value their learning because of the benefits it brings for purposes well beyond their own personal development.

These stories offer insights into how older black women care for others in the community and seek to share purposeful learning. The caring roles are varied and are carried out not only for their immediate and extended family but also the wider community. I have deviated from the brief personal biographies to include details of the studies and previous occupations of these women to demonstrate their long-standing involvement in caring for others.

In the case of the women in Act 7 they point to a phase in which they begin to care for themselves, which occurs when they are largely free from major caring responsibilities and can begin to broaden their horizons and attend to their own personal development. The women refer to such a time as 'spreading our wings' and talk of 'an opportunity for independence and freedom'. The chapter charts journeys through formal learning in later life, initially by highlighting benefits, with experiences of education in the UK, and then by detailing snippets of education they experienced in the Caribbean. Fuller details of the educational dilemmas encountered by the eldest member of the group are described in Chapter 7.

Reflecting on the acts

The acts demonstrated learning in 'womanist' ways to be a source of personal and collective inspiration for lifelong learners and a source of strength in their later lives. They depicted varied stories of learning, informal and formal, as women learning from community-based settings and experiences and through specific programmes. Critical themes such as humiliation, shame, poverty and frustration recur in the stories, relating both to past experiences 'back home' and their years in Britain. The stories revealed barriers to learning, struggles and conflicting demands in their lives but also memories of happier times, of hopes and aspirations.

The acts illustrate the women's positive experiences of recent learning that allowed some of them to spread their wings by pursuing their learning aspirations from informal to non-formal and formal settings. Such aspirations often focus on tackling a particular learning challenge, ultimately bringing satisfaction, elation and contentment. And their learning could help others in their communities; Act 7 especially shows how participating in learning went alongside building social capital. This was facilitated by initiatives such as community teaching and community mentoring networks, which the women saw as helping to improve the quality of life for younger generations. In many areas, they expressed a bond with all the children in the wider black community (Collins, 2000a).

Concluding the Acts

The acts present the women's challenges over issues such as their ethnic identity, their resistance to conformity and labels that I or any outside representative might import. Their version of events had to be an essential component when presenting their stories. Gubrium and Holstein warn that listeners 'respond to a speaker's story with diverse embellishments of their own, which in turn give accounts distinctly experiential and emotional resonance' (Gubrium and Holstein, 2009: 81). As 'Narrator', I attended to these concerns by interspersing narrative interruptions, comments and reflections into the women's accounts so I could make my own role transparent. And narratives, 'in addition to describing what happened, also express emotions, thoughts, and interpretations' (Chase, 2008: 65). While acknowledging that: 'if stories are actively composed, storytelling is staged – it is animated and transpires somewhere in relation to some audience, for some purpose' (Gubrium and Holstein, 2009: 81), I was bound as a contemporary narrative researcher to interpreting the women's narratives responsibly.

Second-wave feminists 'poured new life into the study of personal narratives' (Chase, 2008: 58). This made space for me to adopt a nuanced approach and ensure that the women in my study were 'subjects' rather than 'objects' of the research (ibid.: 62). And while men may be 'distant others' in my research, the lives of black women are at the forefront – both taking part and determining the outcomes – for the benefit of the wider black community.

I concluded that alongside the uniqueness of individual experiences, similarities or commonalities could also be observed in the stories in this book. I have sought to draw out some of the key common themes, applying Chase's (2005) three voices of narrative strategies – authoritative, supportive and interactive – to developing these themes, along with the strategies of narrative analysis described in Chapter 3.

Reproducing the women's exact words allows room for the reader's interpretation (Riessmann, 2002). However, by using narrated acts, I add my 'supportive voice', so as to foreground the women's voices but still maintain the researcher's respectful distance. And my 'interactive voice' was apparent when I listened and intervened. Using my 'authoritative voice' to select material and insert my voice as narrator, I was already building meanings and understanding of the women's stories for a wider audience. Despite aspects of collaboration in the research process, when I then constructed meanings my interests differed from theirs and I distanced myself from the women, whereas during the interviews their voices and emotions had resonated with me.

The black womanist learning matriarch: A catalyst for change

This book has used a contemporary narrative approach to give a theoretical and conceptual account of the learning of older black women who are volunteering in their local communities, and how they benefit from this learning.

The learning I have described appears to have five purposes: for inclusion, for critical consciousness, to enter the mainstream, for social participation and for emancipation. My research has both strengths and limitations, and both have implications for future policy and research. The scenes described show how the women who spoke with me have been subjected to economic hardship and social inequality that is structurally embedded in the societies they came from and the one they subsequently joined, and that create multiple barriers to learning and educational achievement.

This is the first book in the literature on lifelong learning that considers the significance of informal black feminist learning spaces. For these first-generation African Caribbean women these spaces have served to counteract the negative influences of post-colonial, male-dominated teaching environments and instead offer strong bases from which they can pursue wider goals. My concept of matriarchal learning hubs, where black women elders can benefit from informal social learning, contributes a new dimension to the literature, drawing attention to the women's use of powerful shared language, an internal discourse within their polyrhythmic learning realities that motivated them, and anchored their individual and group identities.

The women's stories raise questions about whose knowledge and education are perpetuated through the generations. I show that enabling access to learning is insufficient in itself to ensure inclusion. It is clear that creating the kind of education that neither superimposes knowledge nor is culturally exclusive helps to encourage learning among those who were previously alienated from education. Such settings enable personal development through social participation but they also offer potentially emancipatory contexts. The shared connections established in these informal learning contexts facilitated an increasingly critical consciousness of knowledge and its uses, and the women were able to strengthen their bonds with each other as older black women involved in a collective mission to better themselves – and in many cases, others also – and to address issues in their wider communities.

Older black women learners: A way forward
Learning for inclusion

Inclusion can have both positive and negative connotations; the women's narratives pointed strongly to their desire to access education but also to have control of the terms of inclusion. Not to have control would have reinforced earlier educational exclusion and the deficit model of their learning. My findings uncovered high levels of alienation and exclusion among these women who were taking part in local, strategic community initiatives. I have related their involvement in volunteering, leading to informal learning opportunities that were primarily aimed at benefiting others; these routes became ways to challenge exclusion and engage with learning for inclusion. However, that inclusion was not necessarily in mainstream activities, and many of the women were acutely aware that, in addition to their separate informal (polyrhythmic) learning groups, partnership with other board members and people outside their group was needed if they were to avoid isolation from other mainstream community support networks, and particularly the funding bodies.

While learning for inclusion, the women became aware of the demise of local projects and witnessed growing social problems and inequalities. Maintaining their inclusion involved grouping together to support their sisters by participating in community empowerment initiatives. These included reading and writing groups and health and mentoring projects, where they articulated their views and used their learning to raise critical consciousness (Freire, 1970) more widely in their communities.

The book tells of women who are beginning to trust and support those who are providing much-needed resources and training. But could their involvement have been encouraged as a means of incorporation, so compromising the women's intentions to empower others in their communities? It is important to question who has primarily benefited from the 'empowerment' training made available to the women. Was it the existing board members and local authority, the women themselves, the colleges or perhaps the independent trainers who were given the funds to develop the women's work? If it was it the wider local community who received support from the women, then the women's learning may also have involved development of their critical consciousness.

Learning for critical consciousness

In many cases the women's learning *was* developing their critical consciousness. This was implicit in their purposes: the compromises they made had important and purposive benefits. They were both taking control of their learning and also assuming roles as responsible citizens, in the interests of themselves and of others. According to the women, changes would come when their voices were heard and their views taken seriously but also when the views of others in the community were seen as part of, and included in, the local change-making agenda. Many of the women in the study believed they were playing a useful role, but their social capital and resources were often located within the polyrhythmic learning groups where they were insiders – and yet excluded from the wider community because of their positions on the local boards. However, the women perceived learning as a way of accessing the tools to further represent their communities. The consciousness that accrued from their learning and community activities enabled them to become privileged in their local community positions and as close as possible to understanding local authority agendas.

The women tended to use powerful language, an internal discourse within their polyrhythmic learning realities that served to motivate them, anchoring individual and group identities (Foucault, 1971) and enhancing critical consciousness, though operating at times to exclude others. But while the women were powerful in their informal learning groups, they also gathered information from their membership of community-led government partnerships to share with each other. As long-serving board members they acquired new knowledge from such boards and chose when to share such knowledge with others.

In their polyrhythmic learning groups the women were 'alone–together'. They were able to articulate their learning needs and trust each other. The polyrhythmic learning environments played a vital role, not least in reflecting (on) strategies for critical consciousness. In parallel with American black feminist literature discussed earlier (hooks, 2003), the strengths gained from learning 'alone–together' were crucial in developing the confidence to affect wider changes. If older black women are used to fulfil other, for instance, policy-driven objectives, such as in empowering them with skills as 'good' citizens, questions arise about the nature of empowerment and inclusion, and the extent to which these women could – and can continue to – subvert external purposes to achieve more critical or challenging agendas.

Learning and entering the mainstream

This book assesses the disconnection between older black women learners and the wider research world. It has uncovered an inclusive cultural learning experience in which these learners were seen to have pushed through from the margins of lifelong learning to the mainstream, where they emerged as independent, confident community learners. Most of the women featured in this book struggled at first to find an autonomous place for themselves in their local communities, after previously immersing themselves in what they experienced as male-dominated community projects – often led by radical anti-feminist activists. They talked of having little hope of securing future financial support from a deteriorating 'post-anti-racist' local government grant-giving structure. However, by participating in community initiatives as volunteers, the women seemed to find a place from which to represent others, taking roles as mentors, local board members and tenants' representatives and other prominent roles where learning became the catalyst for change.

Here my research connects with Lave and Wenger's concept of peripheral community participation (1991) discussed earlier, asking whether the women were still closer to the margins or part of a core learning community. The fact that they were separated in their informal matriarchal arenas, away from other projects and participants, could be perceived as problematic. The actual polyrhythmic spaces of learning, however, were not confined to the community learning centres but existed as informal social networks where, in their familiar communities of practice (Wenger, 1998), the women talked *labrish*, made *commess* and took time to *cuss* and scold each other. They challenged, joked and reflected on stories of 'back home', and in the process shared and, importantly, absorbed, new learning. Once learning was acquired by one woman, in these informal situations, it was cascaded and shared with others. Such continual interaction supported the women in fostering greater legitimacy and creating their own learning communities alongside others' communities of practice.

The strategy of separateness within wider communities of practice allowed an effective role to evolve, strengthening strategies toward a successful shift from the margins to a central community role, and enabling the women to put their learning to good use more widely. Learning in this way supported the older women volunteers particularly, and also ensured their control over their learning lives. Their shared common interests, learning together and their collective sense of 'putting something back into their communities' emerged strongly within what I refer to as matriarchal learning settings, as they conveyed what they had learnt to others. In this way the women were creating powerful and separate communities of practice by demonstrating that they were equipped and committed to tackling issues in their communities and that they were also sensitive to supporting the learning aspirations of their peers.

Both 'bonding' and 'bridging' forms of social capital are visibly in play here (Baron *et al.*, 2000). Firstly, the women drew on their social bonds to reinforce their exclusive identities and sustain their close cultural ties as they remained strong and trusting of each other, working closely together in their matriarchal learning hubs. However, the strength of mutual connections potentially denied opportunities for the women to benefit from bridging social capital (Field, 2005), in other words, to network and develop external resources, since there was seldom the chance to participate with people outside the shared cultural spaces they occupied. Thus the women remained outsiders, unable to benefit from the wider resources available to others. Viewed differently, however, a process of extending social and educational resources is visible.

Often 'policy' defines bridging capital as the desirable 'commodity' – to remedy deficits in social capital and in learning. This denies the value of the social bonds for the women in this book, who shared values and ideas in lively polyrhythmic settings. The bonding in partnerships provided arenas to tackle learning challenges, such as the development of confidence in basic literacy and communication skills, in an effort to address a community concern. Volunteering is often assumed to connect with ideas of community bonding, yet the engagement of many women in active voluntary work encouraged them to participate in wider learning and share a desire to effect wider changes, and thence wider societal involvement. Far from representing a deficit model of social resources or a barrier to achievement, their bonding social capital provided an important base and strength for wider learning and in accessing social resources. Simply immersing older black women in learning activities over which they had little control – or that were reminiscent of past alienation – would have offered few opportunities for them to spread their wings.

However, during the course of my research there were already reductions in funding and available community spaces, and as these shortages intensify, those least connected with the local authority decision-makers are likely to lose most. The ability for older black women learners to participate as active citizens in community contexts in the future is threatened, and with it their participation in mainstream learning and community action. Where women in the study found alternative learning venues within their homes, they still relied on their connection with community centres and organizations to ground and disseminate their activities.

Learning in social settings

Black feminist epistemology can assist us in attempting to understand the benefits of lifelong learning for first-generation African Caribbean women (see Chapter 2). This book has revealed the nature and significance of polyrhythmic realities (Sheared, 1999) in the ways in which these women interact and learn together in social settings. Their use of Caribbean patois was frequent and demonstrated confidence as they pursued learning in their womanist ways. While the researcher's own voice was not to be found in the distinct and uniquely Caribbean patois expressed in the women's narratives, it was heard separately, in the narrator's voice embedded in the acts and scenes in which the stories were told.

It is clear that older black women have a commitment to volunteering and helping others in the community, and their shared cultural background and specific experiences meant they were able to work and learn together well. In addition, the symbolic nature of the locations created settings that were familiar and conducive to learning. The locations signified that these were often marginalized activities. But as Lave and Wenger (1991) point out, learning that is embedded in social participation offers important strengths:

namely, the value and comfort of informal learning within a familiar and supportive network, as in the various settings described in this book.

Learning for emancipation: Purposeful matriarchal social learning movements for change

In Chapter 1, I examined the diverse purposes ascribed to lifelong learning and the extent to which these are shaped by policymakers or in alternative ways by learners. I wanted to know whether the different learning activities had benefited or met the purposes of older black women (and if so, which activities). Now I explore the emancipatory potential of their learning activities. My research showed the older black women were engaged in purposeful learning and were consciously aware of this. Their purposes ultimately included emancipation, not only for themselves as people previously disadvantaged in education, but also for the benefit of the community. While many women seemed primarily interested in providing sisterly support to one another and in obtaining qualifications and skills, these often fulfilled an additional aim of helping their community. For example, the women's learning also involved mothers supporting daughters, and the initiatives they chose to get involved in were purposefully emancipatory. Their aims were clear: they wished to build a less dependent future for the next generation of women and foster confident voices. These older black women could be said to care for all the 'black community's children' (Collins, 1990; hooks, 2001). This form of purposeful learning has significant benefits in an ageing society. It is initiated by older matriarchs who pass on skills and unique insights that influence lifestyles in the wider community.

The women's narratives reflected their desire for learning, and the polyrhythmic messages spoken transcended learning in powerful, compelling, lingering assertions of struggle. Womanist politics were apparent in the intentions and the reflective practices of the women when they presented their stories of 'back home', and evident too in the younger of the first-generation African Caribbean women's approaches to personal freedom. Although their discussions did not dwell on overt Western feminism, the 'complex bounded ethnicities' of their varied Caribbean identities (Antrobus, 2004) kept the women focused on a just cause: learning for emancipation of their wider community.

The women's stories of the complexities of identity were laced with lost confidence because of their heritage and their diverse, but predominantly negative, past educational experiences. Complexities of their identity relating to their shades of blackness, Afro-centric and Indo-

Caribbean nuances, coupled with the legacy of slavery, caused pain, shame and hurt and threw up personal barriers to learning. Issues of sexuality were shared only in one-to-one discussions with younger first-generation Caribbean women, who pointed to the unspoken barriers they faced. The women highlighted how learning in local, sometimes fiercely opinionated, women's groups played a key role in helping them to find their voice and break down cultural barriers.

There were tensions between breaking new ground and embedded responsibilities, and these were worked out in complex ways. First-generation African Caribbeans in the study who were mothers, grandmothers and great-grandmothers felt a strong sense of duty to their black communities, beyond their island heritage, although they acknowledged differences among them when they disputed values within their group. Collins (2000a) and Hudson-Weems (2004) discuss this matriarchal responsibility from an African American perspective, but for Caribbean women in the UK it had often been only a notion or aspiration, held over from their former lives in the Caribbean.

However, it was clear that volunteering and learning in their communities had recaptured some of this sense the women had of social responsibility, and that this, coupled with their engagement with learning, became emancipatory for them and for others. According to Jarvis (2007), lifelong learning is often used to underpin emerging social movements and becomes a vehicle to address social issues at community level. The stories I related here support this: we see how some of the women were able to use their learning to contribute to collective changes, while others were furthering aspirations toward empowering others.

The end and the beginning of my own story

After my parents were told by my head teacher that I was aloof and would need 'to expand' my vocabulary if I was to find my way, I had two choices: I could become angry, frustrated and rebellious, like some of my peers, or I could focus on improving my education. I took the latter course and dedicated myself to learning at every opportunity. This was not easy after regularly feeling the wrath of the maths teacher who spent much of her teaching time throwing exercise books at the heads of us poorly performing pupils. Nonetheless, I felt that when one was at the very bottom the only way was up. In secondary school my spare moments away from family chores and responsibilities were spent locked in my room reading. Gradually my school work began to improve. I did not stay at the bottom of the class for long.

Everything changed when I began to receive A grades for English literature. My other subject grades improved too and my teachers began to say pleasant things about me. My mother paid for me to have violin lessons even though she could not really afford it. I hated the violin – the other girls laughed at me, my brothers laughed at me – but I stuck with it because my mother wanted me to learn it. A year later I was chosen as the best-performing pupil in my year and was honoured with a speech day award, and I became good enough at the violin to play in the school orchestra, performing 'Land of Hope and Glory' at Hornsey Town Hall. My parents attended and were proud as they witnessed me walk across the stage to receive my prize from the officials. For them this was a milestone but for me it was to be the beginning of a most fruitful learning journey.

There were four class streams in our secondary school, 1AZ to 1AW, and I desperately wanted to get to 1AW. I never did make it but I left secondary school with CSEs, O levels and A levels, in English literature and art. I wanted to pursue a further a A level so I could go to university but my parents would not hear of it. I had to go out to work to help pay the household bills. By that time my mother had an extra job at the Town Hall cleaning the offices of the Borough Engineer. She spoke with him and soon I was being interviewed for my first job in local government. Until I finally left home and the protective clutches of my mother, my desire for increased levels of formal education was placed on hold. My glass was half empty and I was determined that one day I would have the freedom to learn. And so I shared with the women I met for this study and this book the desire for learning in my later years. In Chapter 1 I referred to the 'beginning of my own story' and to the 'disappointment on the faces of the long-serving grammar school teachers as they were compelled to teach large numbers of underperforming learners'. In connecting the end and the beginning of my own story I am mindful of the fact that, while staff members probably never forgave us for lowering the standards of their pristine former grammar school, they threw out a challenge that helped propel me to the University of Bristol and eventually break through all the barriers that had stood in the way of my educational desires.

And so I end this book by calling on academics, practitioners and policymakers to prepare well for the flourishing groups of older, more active women learners who still have a desire for learning to equip them with skills to make a constructive difference to their lives and to the lives of others around them. To the future funders of public, voluntary and community sector services, I say: community learning spaces matter. For diverse groups of older women learners, such spaces are vital for volunteering, enriching lives and increasing social capital, happiness and wellbeing in depressed urban black communities. Finally, as the black women in my study so strongly illustrate, we have a valuable contribution to make in promoting lifelong learning in womanist ways. Whether learners or teachers, we pass on the baton to future generations as we pursue and value the freedom to learn and make a difference in our later years.

Glossary of Caribbean patois terms

Term/Expression	Meaning	Used by
Anancy	Caribbean folk stories	Barbara
bacchanal	Wild and lively Caribbean revelling	Merlina
bobolos	A swindler	Trudy
buppies	Young, black and upwardly mobile	Vereen
buss up shut	Trinidadian-style flat roti bread	Maxine
commess	Noisy tittle-tattle; lively, disruptive gatherings	Cynthia
Cou Cou and flying fish	Often considered the national dish of Barbados	Anne-Marie
doubles	Fried flat breads with chickpeas	Merlina
Dougla	A mixed Caribbean person of African and Indian–Asian descent	Shirley
duppy	Jamaican slang for ghost or spirit	Deloris
facety	West Indian slang – meaning cheeky or rude	Mary
hickass	Jovial cuss word often meaning 'serves you right'	Anselma
jinal	A trickster	Deloris
koshoni	Nonsense or stupidity	Anselma
labrish	Gossip or chit chat	Alphena
liming	Hanging out, joking and laughing with friends	Mindy
malpop	Selfish, conceited, nasty person	Anselma
mamaguise	Tricks to deceive others – often played out by Caribbean matriarchs	Alphena
margee	Foolishness or rubbish	Anselma
obeah	A form of Caribbean black magic or witchcraft with roots in religious practices developed among West African slaves	Eldra

Term/Expression	Meaning	Used by
Playing mas	Having fun, masquerading and dancing in the streets	Merlina
Ro-ro	Excitement, commotion and scandalous talk	Anselma
runnings	Goings on; people's confrontations, events and activities	Cindy
sakafet	A common Creole greeting that means 'How are you?'	Alphena
salop	Swear word	Anselma
vesearse	Pretending to like someone or something; vain or self-centred	Rosamond

Other terms

First-generation African Caribbean women: Black women who came to the UK in large numbers in the 1950s and 1960s from a variety of Caribbean islands.

In search of our carnival spirits: An expression of new-found freedom but also a yearning for an earlier, more frivolous life for first-generation African Caribbean women.

Older African Caribbean women: In this book, 'older' refers to women aged 50 and over.

'The heart of the race': This chapter title is taken from the publication (Bryan *et al.*, 1985) of the same name that explores black women's lives in Britain.

'A touch of class': The title of this act is taken from the work of Maguire (1999).

References

Abrams, B.A. (2010) *Acculturation and its Effect on Afro-Caribbean Mother–Daughter Relationships*. Miami: Miami University.

Adelson, K. (2000) 'Lifelong learning and voluntary organisations'. In Field, J. and Leicester, M. (eds) *Lifelong Learning*. London: RoutledgeFalmer.

Afshar, H., Franks, M., Maynard, M. and Wray, S. (2002a) 'Issues in ethnicity in researching older women'. *Growing Older Programme ESRC Newsletter*, Spring.

— (2002b) 'Gender, ethnicity and empowerment in later life'. *Quality in Ageing Journal*, 3 (1), 27–33.

Aldridge, F. and Tuckett, A. (2002) *Two Steps Forward, One Step Back: The NIACE survey on adult participation in learning*. Leicester: NIACE.

Alfred, M.V. (2002) 'The politics of knowledge and theory construction in adult education: A critical analysis from an Africentric feminist perspective'. *New Directions for Adult and Continuing Education, 96*, 3–14.

— (2003) 'Sociocultural contexts and learning: Anglophone Caribbean immigrant women in US postsecondary education'. *Adult Education Quarterly*, 53 (4), 242–60.

— (2006) 'Race, politics and economic self-sufficiency in a culture of welfare reform'. In Merriam, S., Courtenay, B. and Cervero, R. (eds) *Global Issues and Adult Education: Perspectives from Latin America, Southern Africa, and the United States*. San Francisco, CA: Jossey-Bass.

— (2009) 'Social capital theory and adult learning'. In Nanton, C. and Alfred, M.V. (eds) *Social Capital and Women's Support System: Networking, learning, and surviving*. San Francisco, CA: Jossey-Bass.

Amos, V. and Parmar, P. (1984) 'Challenging imperial feminism'. *Feminist Review,* 17, 3–19.

Andaiye, A. (2002) 'The angle you look from determines what you see: Towards a critique of feminist politics in the Caribbean'. The Lucille Mathurin Mair Lecture, Centre for Gender and Development Studies, University of the West Indies.

Angelou, M. (1978) *Still I Rise*. New York, NY: Random.

Annette, J. and Mayo, M. (2009) 'Active learning for active citizenship: Democratic citizenship and lifelong learning'. *Education, Citizenship and Social Justice*, 4 (2), 149–60.

Antrobus, P. (2004) *The Global Women's Movement: Origins, issues and strategies*. London: Zed Press.

Ardelt, M. (2000) 'Intellectual versus wisdom-related knowledge: The case for a different kind of learning in the later years of life'. *Educational Gerontology, International Journal of Research and Practice*, 26 (8), 771–89.

Bailey, B. and Leo-Rhynie, E. (2004) *Gender in the 21ˢᵗ Century: Caribbean perspectives, visions and possibilities*. Kingston, Jamaica: Randle.

Baksh-Soodeen, R. (1994) 'Caribbean feminism in international perspective'. *Economic and Political Weekly*, 29 (44), 50–6.

Barnes, M., Newman, J. and Sullivan, H. (2007) *Power, Participation and Political Renewal: Case studies in public participation.* Bristol: Policy Press.

Baron, S., Field, J. and Schuller, T. (2000) *Social Capital: Critical perspectives.* Oxford: Oxford University Press.

Barriteau, E. (2004) 'Constructing feminist knowledge in the commonwealth Caribbean in the era of globalization'. In Bailey, B. and Leo-Rhynie, E. (eds) *Gender in the 21st Century: Caribbean perspectives, visions and possibilities.* Kingston, Jamaica: Ian Randle Publishers.

— (2007) 'The relevance of black feminist scholarship: A Caribbean perspective'. *Feminist Africa: Diaspora Voices*, 7, 9–31.

Baumgartner, L.M and Johnson-Bailey, J. (2010) 'A field of flowers and broken glass'. In Jackson, S. (ed.) *Innovations in Lifelong Learning: Critical perspectives on diversity, participation and vocational learning.* London: Routledge.

Bell, J.S. (2002) 'Narrative inquiry: More than just telling stories'. *TESOL Quarterly*, 36 (2), 207–13.

Bennett, L. (1982) *Selected Poems: Louise Bennett.* Kingston, Jamaica: Sangsters.

Better Government for Older People (BGOP) (2000) *All Our Futures: The report of the Better Government for Older People Steering Committee.* London: BGOP.

Bhavnani, K.K. (2001) *Feminism & 'Race'.* Oxford: Oxford University Press.

Biesta, G. (2012) 'Have lifelong learning and emancipation still something to say to each other?' *Studies in the Education of Adults*, 44 (1), 5–20.

Binta Breeze, J. (1988) *Ryddim Ravings and Other Poems.* London: Race Today.

Bostrom, A. (2002) 'Informal learning in a formal context: Problematizing the concept of social capital in a contemporary Swedish context'. *International Journal of Lifelong Education*, 21 (6), 510–24.

Brah, A. and Phoenix, A. (2004) 'Ain't I a woman? Revisiting intersectionality'. *Journal of International Women's Studies*, 5 (3), 75–86.

Brent, J. (2009) *Searching for Community: Representation, power and action on an urban estate.* Bristol: Policy Press.

Bryan, B., Dadzie, S. and Scafe, S. (1985) *The Heart of the Race: Black women's lives in Britain.* London: Virago Press.

Burke, P. and Jackson, S. (2007) *Reconceptualising Lifelong Learning: Feminist interventions.* London: Routledge.

Butt, J. and O'Neil, A. (2004) *'Let's move on': Black and minority ethnic older people's views on research findings.* York: Joseph Rowntree Foundation.

Campbell, C. and McLean, C. (2002) *Ethnic Identity, Social Capital and Health: Factors shaping African Caribbean participation in local community networks.* London: LSE.

Carby, H.V. (1997) 'White women listen! Black women and the boundaries of sisterhood'. In Mirza, H.S. (ed.) *Black British Feminism.* London: Routledge.

Chase, S.E. (1996) 'Personal vulnerability and interpretive authority in narrative research'. In Josselson, R. (ed.) *Ethics and Process in the Narrative Study of Lives.* Thousand Oaks, CA: Sage Publications.

— (2003) 'Learning to listen: Narrative principles in a qualitative research methods course'. In Josselson, R., Lieblich, A. and McAdams, D.P. (eds) *Up Close and Personal: The teaching and learning of narrative research.* Washington, DC: American Psychological Association.

— (2008) 'Narrative inquiry: Multiple lenses, approaches, voices'. In Denzin, N.K. and Lincoln, Y.S. (eds) *Collecting and Interpreting Qualitative Materials*. Thousand Oaks, CA: Sage Publications.

Christian, B. (1988) 'The race for theory'. *Feminist Studies,* 14 (1), 67–79.

Clandinin, D.J. (ed.) (2006) *Handbook of Narrative Inquiry: Mapping a methodology*. Thousand Oaks, CA: Sage Publications.

Clayton, P.M. (1995) 'Ethnic minorities and adult education: Some developments in Greater Glasgow'. *Adult Education for a Multi-cultural Society*. Proceedings of a conference at the Queen's University of Belfast, 19 May.

— (2006) *Vocational Guidance and Inclusion in Lifelong Learning*. Glasgow: University of Glasgow Department of Continuing Education.

Coffield, F. (ed.) (1997) *A National Strategy for Lifelong Learning*. Newcastle-upon-Tyne: University of Newcastle Department of Education.

Colley, H., Hodkinson, P. and Malcolm, J. (2002) *Non-formal Learning: Mapping the conceptual terrain – a consultation report*. Leeds: University of Leeds Lifelong Learning Institute.

Collins, P.H. (1990) *Black Feminist Thought: Knowledge, consciousness and the politics of empowerment*. London: Routledge.

— (2000a) 'The social construction of black feminist thought'. In Bhavnani, K.K. (ed.) *Feminism and 'Race'*. Oxford: Oxford University Press.

— (2000b) 'What's going on? Black feminist thought and the politics of postmodernism'. In St Pierre, E. and Pillow, W. (eds) *Working the Ruins: Feminist poststructural theory and methods in education*. New York: Routledge.

Connelly, F.M. and Clandinin, D.J. (1999) 'Narrative inquiry'. In Keeves, J.P. and Lakomski, G. (eds) *Issues in Educational Research*. New York, NY: Pergamon Press.

— (2006) 'Narrative inquiry'. In Green, J., Camilli, G. and Elmore, P. (eds) *Handbook of Complementary Methods in Education Research*. Mahwah, NJ: Lawrence Erlbaum.

Cooper, A.J.H. (1988) *A Voice from the South: By a black woman of the south*. New York, NY: Oxford University Press.

Corbin, J. and Strauss, A. (2008) *Basics of Qualitative Research*. 3rd ed. London: Sage Publications.

Crick, B. (2000a) *Essays on Citizenship*. London: Continuum.

— (2000b) *Education for Democratic Citizenship*. London: Department for Education and Employment.

Cropley, A.J. (1980) *Towards a System of Lifelong Learning: Some practical considerations*. Hamburg: UNESCO.

Crowther, J. (2004) 'In and against lifelong learning: Flexibility and the corrosion of character'. *International Journal of Lifelong Education*, 23 (2), 125–36.

Cullen, J., Batterbury, S., Foresti, M., Lyons, C. and Stern, E. (2000) *Informal Learning and Widening Participation*. DfEE Research Report No. 191. London: Tavistock Institute.

Czarniawska, B. (2004) *Narratives in Social Science Research*. London: Sage Publications.

Dadzie, S. (1993) *'Older and Wiser': A study of educational provision for black and ethnic minority elders*. Leicester: NIACE.

Denzin, N.K. (1989a) *Interpretive Biography*. Newbury Park, CA: Sage Publications.

— (1989b) *The Research Act: A theoretical introduction to sociological methods*. Englewood Cliffs, NJ: Prentice Hall.

Doukas, C. (2002) 'New topologies in European policies: The framework of lifelong learning policies'. In Medel-Añonuevo, C. (ed.) *Lifelong Learning Discourses in Europe*. Hamburg: UNESCO Institute for Education.

Dove, N. (1998) 'Africana womanism: An Afrocentric theory'. *Journal of Black Studies*, 28 (5), 515–39.

Dunnell, K. (2007) *Diversity and Different Experiences in the UK: National statistician's annual report on society*. London: Office for National Statistics.

Earthy, S. and Cronin, A. (2008) 'Narrative analysis'. In Gilbert, N. (ed.) *Researching Social Life*. Thousand Oaks, CA: Sage Publications.

Eaton K.C. (2007) *Womanism, Literature, and the Transformation of the Black Community, 1965–1980*. Abingdon: Routledge.

Ellis, P. (ed.) (1985) *Women of the Caribbean*. London: Zen.

Etienne, J. and Jackson, S. (2010) 'Beyond the home: Informal learning and community participation for older women'. In Jackson, S. (ed.) *Innovations in Lifelong Learning: Critical perspectives on diversity, participation and vocational learning*. Abingdon: Routledge.

— (2011) 'Lifelong learning in later years: Choices and constraints for older women'. In Jackson, S., Malcolm, I. and Thomas, K. (eds) *Gendered Choices: Learning, work, identities in lifelong learning*. Dordrecht: Kluwer Academic Press.

Evandrou, M. (2000) 'Social inequalities in later life: The socio-economic position of older people from ethnic minority groups in Britain'. *Population Trends*, 101, 11–18.

Field, J. (2003) *Researching Lifelong Learning: Trends and prospects in the English-speaking world*. Stirling, Scotland: University of Stirling.

— (2005) *Social Capital and Lifelong Learning*. Bristol: Policy Press.

— (2006a) *Lifelong Learning and the New Educational Order*. Stoke-on-Trent: Trentham Books.

— (2006b) 'Has lifelong learning had its day?' *Adults Learning*, 17 (8), 16–17.

Field, J. and Spence, L. (2000) 'Informal learning and social capital'. In Coffield, F. (ed.) *The Necessity of Informal Learning*. Bristol: Policy Press.

Foucault, M. (1971) *The Order of Things*. London: Tavistock.

— (1980) *Power/Knowledge*. New York, NY: Pantheon.

Frank, D. (ed.) (2001) *Kweyol Dictionary*. Castries, St Lucia: Ministry of Education.

Franzosi, R. (1998) 'Narrative Analysis – Or Why (and How) Sociologists Should be Interested in Narrative'. *Annual Review of Sociology*, 24, 517-54.

Freire, P. (1970) *Pedagogy of the Oppressed*. Harmondsworth: Penguin.

— (1972) *Cultural Action for Freedom*. Harmondsworth: Penguin.

— (1999) *Pedagogy of Hope*. New York, NY: Continuum.

Fryer, R.H. (2008) *Lifelong Learning, Citizenship and Belonging: A briefing paper prepared for the Independent Commission of Inquiry on the Future of Lifelong Learning*. Leicester: NIACE.

Gabriel, D. (2007) *Layers of Blackness: Colonialism in the African diaspora*. London: Imani Media Ltd.

Garmanikow, E. and Green, A. (1999) 'Developing social capital: Dilemmas, possibilities and limitations in education'. In Hayton, A. (ed.) *Tackling Disaffection and Social Exclusion: Education, policies and perspectives*. London: Kogan Page.

Gilbert, N. (2008) *Researching Social Life*. London: Sage Publications.

Gillborn, D. (2006) 'Critical race theory and education: Racism and anti-racism in educational theory and praxis'. *Discourse: Studies in the Cultural Politics of Education*, 27 (1), 11–32.

Gillham, B. (2005) *Research Interviewing: The range of techniques*. Maidenhead: Open University Press.

Gorard, S. (2000) 'Robbing Peter to pay Paul: Resolving the contradiction of lifelong learning'. Research in Post-Compulsory Education, 7 (2), 123–32.

Goulbourne, H. and Chamberlain, M. (eds) (2001) *Caribbean Families in Britain and the Trans-atlantic World*. London: Palgrave.

Gregory, S.T. (2001) 'Black faculty women in the academy: History, status, and future'. *Journal of Negro Education*, 70 (3), 124–38.

Griffin, C (2000) 'Lifelong learning: Policy, strategy and culture'. In *Working Papers of the Global Colloquium on Supporting Lifelong Learning Journal*. Milton Keynes: Open University.

Gubrium, J.F. and Holstein, J.A. (eds) (2001) *Institutional Selves: Troubled identities in a post-modern world*. New York, NY: Oxford University Press.

— (2009) *Analyzing Narrative Reality*. Thousand Oaks, CA: Sage Publications.

Hall, S. (1992) 'New ethnicities'. In Donald, J. and Rattansi, A. (eds) *'Race', Culture & Difference*. London: Sage Publications.

Hertz, R. (ed.) (1997) *Reflexivity and Voice*. Thousand Oaks, CA: Sage Publications.

Hills, J., Brewer, M., Jenkins, S., Lister, R., Lupton, R., Machin, S., Mills, C., Modood, T., Rees, T. and Riddell, S. (2010) *An Anatomy of Economic Inequality in the UK: Report of the National Economic Panel*. London: Government Equalities Office.

Hoggett, P. (1997) *Contested Communities: Experiences, struggles and policies*. Bristol: Policy Press.

Hollingsworth, S. and Dybdahl, M. (2007) 'Talking to learn: The critical role of conversation in narrative inquiry'. In Clandinin, D.J. (ed.) *Handbook of Narrative Inquiry: Mapping a methodology*. Thousand Oaks, CA: Sage Publications.

Holstein, J.A. and Gubrium, F. (1998) *The Active Interview*. Thousand Oaks, CA: Sage.

hooks, b. (1989) *Talking Back: Thinking feminist, thinking black*. Boston, MA: South End Press.

— (1994) *Teaching to Transgress: Education as the practice of freedom*. London: Routledge.

— (2001) 'Black women: Shaping feminist theory'. In Bhavnani, K.K (ed.) *Feminism and 'Race'*. Oxford: Oxford University Press.

— (2003) *Teaching Community: A pedagogy of hope*. New York, NY: Routledge.

Hudson-Weems, C. (1998) 'Africana womanism: Reclaiming ourselves'. In Nnaemeka, O. (ed.) *Sisterhood, Feminisms and Power: From Africa to the diaspora*. Trenton, NJ: Africa World Press.

— (2004) *Africana Womanist Literary Theory*. Trenton, NJ: Africa World Press.

Institute for Volunteering Research (IVR) (2004) *Volunteering for All? Exploring the link between volunteering and social exclusion*. London: IVR.

Jackson, S. (2005) 'When learning comes of age? Continuing education into later life'. *Journal of Adult and Continuing Education*, 11 (2), 188–99.

— (2006) 'Jam, Jerusalem and Calendar Girls? Lifelong learning and the WI'. *Studies in the Education of Adults*, 38 (1), 74–90.

— (2007) *Learning Citizenship: Lifelong learning, community and the Women's Institute*. ESRC end of award report. Swindon: ESRC.

Jaggi, M. (2000) 'The final passage'. In Owusu, K. (ed.) *Black British Culture and Society*. London: Routledge.

James, C. (2004) *Searching for Anansi: From orature to literature in the West Indian children's folk tradition: Jamaican and Trinidadian trends*. Trinidad: University of the West Indies.

Jamieson, A. (2007) 'Education and the quality of life in later years'. *Quality in Ageing*, 8 (3), 15–23.

Jarvis, P. (2007) *Globalisation, Lifelong Learning and the Learning Society*. London: Routledge.

Johnson-Bailey, J. and Alfred, M.V. (2006) 'Transformational teaching and the practices of black adult educators'. *New Directions for Adult and Continuing Education*, 109, 49–58.

Jones, C. (1952) 'An end to the neglect of the problems of the Negro Woman!' In Meire, A. and Rudwick, C. (eds) *From Plantation to Ghetto: 1915–1954*. London: Constable.

Jones, P. (2010) *Participation in Adult Learning*. London: Equality and Human Rights Commission.

Joseph Rowntree Foundation (2007) *Poverty Rates among Ethnic Groups in Great Britain*. Findings 2057. York: Joseph Rowntree Foundation.

Kilpatrick, S., Field, J. and Falk, I. (2003) 'Social capital: An analytical tool for exploring lifelong learning and community development'. *British Educational Research Journal*, 29 (3), 417–33.

Lave, J. (2001) *Situated Learning: Legitimate peripheral participation*. Revised. Cambridge: Cambridge University Press.

Lave, J. and Wenger, E. (1991) *Situated Learning: Legitimate peripheral participation*. Cambridge: Cambridge University Press.

Lewis, G. (2001) 'Black women's employment and the British economy'. In Kum-Kum, B. (ed.) *Feminism and Race*. Oxford: Oxford University Press.

Lieblich, A. (1996) 'Some unforeseen outcomes of conducting narrative research with people of one's own culture'. In Josselson, R. (ed.) *Ethics and Process in the Narrative Study of Lives*. Thousand Oaks, CA: Sage.

Lievesley, N. (2010) *The Future Ageing of the Ethnic Minority Population in England and Wales*. London: Runnymede and the Centre for Policy on Ageing.

Lorde, A. (1984) *Sister Outsider: Essays and speeches by Audre Lorde*. Berkeley, CA: Crossing Press.

Maguire, M. (1999) 'A touch of class: Inclusion and exclusion in initial teacher education'. *International Journal of Inclusive Education*, 3 (1), 13–26.

May, V.M. (2007) *Anna Julia Cooper, Visionary Black Feminist: A critical introduction*. Abingdon: Routledge.

Maynard, M. (2002) 'Studying age, race and gender: Translating a research proposal into a project'. *International Journal of Social Research Methodology*, 5 (1), 31–40.

— (2003) *Older Women's Lives*. York: University of York.

Maynard, M., Afshar, H., Franks, M. and Wray, S. (2008) *Women in Later Life: Exploring race and ethnicity*. Maidenhead: Open University Press.

Mayo, M. (2000) 'Learning for active-citizenship: Training for and learning from participation in area regeneration'. *Studies in the Education of Adults*, 32 (1), 22–35.

Mayo, M. and Annette, J. (2010) *Taking Part? Active learning for active citizenship, and beyond*. Leicester: NIACE.

McCabe, A., Gilchrist, A., Harris, K., Afridi, A. and Kyprianou, P. (2013) *Making the Links: Poverty, ethnicity and social networks*. York: Joseph Rowntree Foundation.

McGivney, V. (1999) *Informal Learning in the Community: A trigger for change and development*. Leicester: NIACE.

McNair, S. (2009) *Demography and Lifelong Learning: IFLL thematic paper 1*. Leicester: NIACE.

Milbourne, L. (2002) 'Unspoken exclusion: Experiences of continued marginalisation from education among "hard to reach" groups of adults and children'. *British Journal of Sociology of Education*, 23 (2), 287–305.

— (2009) 'Remodelling the third sector: Advancing collaboration or competition in community-based initiatives?' *Journal of Social Policy*, 38 (2), 277–97.

— (2013) *Voluntary Sector in Transition: Hard times or new opportunities?* Bristol: Policy Press.

Mirza, H.S. (ed.) (1997) *Black British Feminism*. London: Routledge.

— (2003) 'All the women are white, all the blacks are men – but some of us are brave: Mapping the consequences of invisibility for black and minority ethnic women in Britain'. In Mason, D. (ed.) *Explaining Ethnic Differences: Changing patterns of disadvantage in Britain*. Bristol: Policy Press.

— (2009) *Race, Gender and Educational Desire: Why black women succeed and fail*. London: Routledge.

Morgan-Klein, B. and Osborne, M. (2007) *The Concepts and Practices of Lifelong Learning*. London: Routledge.

Murray, U. (2011) 'Re-asserting a relational model of teaching and learning: A gender perspective'. In Jackson, S., Malcolm, I. and Thomas, K. (eds) *Gendered Choices: Learning, work, identities in lifelong learning*. Dordrecht: Kluwer Academic Press.

National Institute of Adult Continuing Education (NIACE) (2005) *Cultural Diversity: Responding to the learning needs of older people from black and minority ethnic communities*. Leicester: National Institute of Adult Continuing Education. Now the Learning and Work Institute.

— (2007) *The Future for Lifelong Learning: A national strategy.* Leicester: National Institute of Adult and Continuing Education. Now the Learning and Work Institute.

Ntiri, D.W. (2001) 'Reassessing Africana womanism: Continuity and change'. *The Western Journal of Black Studies,* 25 (3), 168–76.

Paine, A.E., Hill, M. and Rochester, C. (2010) *A Rose by Any Other Name... Revisiting the Question: 'What exactly is volunteering?'* Working paper series: Paper one. London: Institute for Volunteering Research.

Parmar, P. (1990) 'Black feminism: The politics of articulation'. In Rutherford, J. (ed.) *Identity, Community, Culture and Difference.* London: Lawrence & Wishart.

Phoenix, A. (1994) 'Practicing feminist research: The intersection of gender and "race" in the research process'. In Maynard, M. and Purvis, J. (eds) *Researching Women's Lives from a Feminist Perspective.* London: Taylor & Francis.

Platt, L. (2007) *Poverty Rates and Ethnicity in the UK.* Bristol: Policy Press for the Joseph Rowntree Foundation.

Putnam, R.D. (2000) *Bowling Alone: The collapse and revival of American community.* New York, NY: Simon & Schuster.

Reddock, R. (2007) 'Diversity, difference and Caribbean feminism: The challenge of anti-racism'. *Caribbean Review of Gender Studies,* 1, 1–24.

Reynolds, T. (2002) 'Re-thinking a black feminist standpoint'. *Journal of Ethnic and Racial Studies,* 26 (3), 591–600.

— (2005) *Caribbean Mothers: Identity and experience in the UK.* London: Tufnell.

Riessman, C.K. (2001) 'Narrative analysis'. In Lewis-Beck, M.S., Bryman, A. and Liao, T.F. (eds) *The Sage Encyclopedia of Social Science Research Methods: Volume 3.* Thousand Oaks, CA: Sage Publications.

— (2002) 'Doing justice: Positioning the interpreter in narrative work'. In Patterson, W. (ed.) *Strategic Narrative: New perspectives on the power of personal and cultural storytelling.* Lanham, MA: Lexington.

Rollock, N. (2011) 'Unspoken rules of engagement: Navigating racial microaggressions in the academic terrain'. *International Journal of Qualitative Studies in Education,* 25 (5), 517–32.

Schuller, T. (2000) 'Thinking about social capital'. Paper presented at the Festival of Lifelong Learning Conference, University of East London.

Schuller, T. and Field, J. (1998) 'Social capital, human capital and the learning society'. In Edwards, R., Miller, N., Small, N. and Tait, A. (eds) *Supporting Lifelong Learning: Volume 3, making policy work.* Buckinghamshire: Open University Press.

Schuller, T. and Watson, D. (2009) *Learning through Life: Inquiry into the future for lifelong learning – summary.* Leicester: NIACE.

Schuller, T., Preston, N., Hammond, C., Brasset-Grundy, A. and Bynner, J. (2004) *The Benefits of Learning: The impact of education on health, family life and social capital.* London: RoutledgeFalmer.

Sen, A. (2000) *Social Exclusion: Concept, application, and scrutiny. Social Development Papers 1.* Manila: Asian Development Bank.

Sheared, V. (1996) 'An Africentric feminist perspective on the role of adult education for diverse communities'. Paper presented at the International Adult & Continuing Education Conference. Online. http://files.eric.ed.gov/fulltext/ED401417.pdf (accessed 26 January 2016).

— (1999) 'Giving voice: Inclusion of African American students' polyrhythmic realities in adult basic education'. In Guy, T.C. (ed.) *Providing Culturally Relevant Adult Education: A challenge for the twenty first century.* San Francisco, CA: Jossey-Bass.

Sin, C.H. (2004) 'Sampling minority ethnic older people in Britain'. *Ageing and Society,* 24 (2), 257–77.

Smith, B. (ed.) (2000) *Home Girls: A black feminist anthology.* New Brunswick, NJ: Rutgers University Press.

Smith, D., Chaturvedi, N., Harding, S., Nazroo, J. and Williams, R. (2000) 'Ethnic inequality in health: A review of UK epidemiological evidence'. *Critical Public Health,* 10 (4), 375–408.

Soulsby, J. (2000) *Learning in the Fourth Age.* Leicester: NIACE.

Sudbury, J. (1998) *Other Kinds of Dreams: Black women's organisations and the politics of transformation.* London and New York, NY: Routledge.

Sultana, F. (2007) 'Reflexivity, positionality and participatory ethics: Negotiating fieldwork dilemmas in International Research'. *ACME: International E-Journal for Critical Geographies,* 6 (3), 374–385.

Sutherland, M.E. (2006) 'African-Caribbean immigrants in the United Kingdom: The legacy of racial disadvantages'. *Caribbean Quarterly,* 52 (1), 26–52.

Taylor, E., Gillborn, D. and Ladson-Billings, G. (eds) (2009) *Foundations of Critical Race Theory in Education.* New York, NY: Routledge.

Tuckett, A. and McCauley, A. (2005) *Demography and Older Learners: Approaches to a new policy challenge.* Leicester: NIACE.

Walker, A. (1982) *The Color Purple.* San Diego, CA: Harcourt.

— (1983) *In Search of our Mother's Gardens: Womanist prose.* London: The Women's Press.

Wenger, E. (1998) *Communities of Practice: Learning, meaning, and identity.* Cambridge: Cambridge University Press.

Withnall, A. (2000) *Older Learners: Issues and perspectives: Working papers of the global colloquium on supporting lifelong learning.* Milton Keynes: Open University.

— (2002) *Older People and Lifelong Learning: Choices and experiences.* Extending Quality of Life Programme. London: ESRC.

— (2003) 'Reflections on lifelong learning and the third age'. In Field, J. and Leicester, M. (eds.) *Lifelong learning: Education across the lifespan.* London: RoutledgeFalmer.

— (2006) 'Exploring influences on later life learning'. *International Journal for Lifelong Learning,* 25 (1), 29–49.

Young, M. (1971) *Knowledge and Control.* London: Collier Macmillan.

Index